D0919756

And When You
Pray

And When You Pray

The Deeper Meaning *of the* Lord's Prayer

Ray Pritchard

Nashville, Tennessee

0-8054-2342-7

Published by Broadman & Holman Publishers,
Nashville, Tennessee

Dewey Decimal Classification: 226
Subject Heading: PRAYER

Library of Congress Cataloging-in-Publication Data

Pritchard, Ray, 1952–
And when you pray : the deeper meaning of the Lord's prayer / Ray Pritchard.
p. cm.
Includes bibliographical references.
ISBN 0-8054-2342-7
1. Lord's prayer. I. Title.

BV230 .P75 2002
226.9'606—dc21

2001037953

1 2 3 4 5 6 7 8 9 10 06 05 04 03 02

Dedicated to

Ken Aycock
Jeff Hargett
Butch Henderson
Ricky Kirkpatrick
Neil Jones
Paul Lynch
Jeff McAllister
Phil Newton
Rick Suddith
Bruce Thorn

Friends for life

CONTENTS

THE LORD'S PRAYER

Matthew 6:9–13

This, then, is how you should pray:
Our Father in heaven,
hallowed be your name,
your kingdom come,
your will be done
on earth as it is in heaven.
Give us today our daily bread.
Forgive us our debts,
as we also have forgiven our debtors.
And lead us not into temptation,
but deliver us from the evil one,
For yours is the kingdom and the power
and the glory forever. Amen.

INTRODUCTION

THIS IS NOT A BOOK ABOUT PRAYER. It may look like a book about prayer but it isn't, and if that's what you are looking for, you might be happier if you looked somewhere else. I know that's an odd way to introduce a book I hope you'll buy and read and maybe even buy another copy for a friend. But I believe in truth in advertising, so I have to tell you that this isn't a book about how to pray or about the specifics or mechanics of prayer. There are many fine books on those topics, but this isn't one of them. As much as I appreciate those books, I don't feel qualified to write a book like that.

So what is this book all about? This is a book about the greatest prayer in the Bible—the Lord's Prayer. Jesus gave us this prayer as an invitation to take a personal journey to the heart of God. If you have longed to know God and to touch the heart of your Heavenly Father, this is the prayer for you.

I am a bit embarrassed to admit that for many years I did not take the Lord's Prayer seriously. I suppose it is partly because I did not grow up in a church where the Lord's Prayer was a central part of our worship. But there is a deeper problem. Most of us have known the Lord's Prayer since childhood, but we have never examined it closely for ourselves. Consequently, we have either ignored it altogether (as in my case), or we have repeated it without understanding (as in the case of many others). That's a great loss, because the Lord's Prayer is the central prayer of the Christian faith. It is the only prayer our Lord ever taught his disciples to pray. Everything we need to pray about can be found in that prayer. If it's not in there somewhere, then we probably don't need to be praying about it.

I hope this book leads you back to the Lord's Prayer and, through that prayer, back to the heart of God. The subtitle says that we are going to examine "the deeper meaning" of the Lord's Prayer. My goal is not to give you an exhaustive explanation of each phrase. Instead, I want us to discover together how practical and down-to-earth this prayer is. It is timeless in that it has a message for every generation. It is contemporary in that it speaks forcefully to life in the twenty-first century. Every phrase, and even every word, matters. There is nothing extra, no window dressing, no fluffy phrases thrown in to make the prayer sound pious. This is Christian prayer, stripped down to its bare essence, as taught by Jesus Christ. It can be recited in less than a minute. The words are plain, unadorned, and majestic in their simplicity. Here is a prayer suited for the smallest child yet challenging to the greatest minds. We will never come to the end of all that the Lord's Prayer has to teach us.

There are a number of ways to use this book. I think you'll benefit most if you study it with a friend or in a small group. As iron sharpens iron, your friends will have insights you may miss, and you may discover truth they don't see. Even if you read this by yourself, please take time to think about the questions at the beginning and end of each chapter. Don't feel that you have to hurry through the book. Take time to read each chapter, and then take time to pray. You'll probably gain more if you don't try to read it all at one time. The Lord's Prayer is more suited to a leisurely stroll than to a hundred-yard dash. Feel free to underline the text and to jot down questions in the margin. This is your book, and I want it to help you.

Once again I have found great encouragement from Len Goss of Broadman & Holman Publishers. I owe special thanks to David and ClarLyn Morris. This is the third time they loaned me their cottage on the Fox River so I could have a quiet place to write. And I am especially grateful to my wife, Marlene, and to my three boys, Josh, Mark, and Nick, for giving me everything that makes life worth living.

It's time to get started on our journey to the heart of God. Let's step back twenty centuries and listen in as Jesus teaches his disciples how to pray.

"This, then,
is how you should pray."
MATTHEW 6:9

CHAPTER ONE

INVITATION TO THE HEART OF GOD

Before we begin: How old were you when you first learned the Lord's Prayer? How often do you pray the Lord's Prayer? Why does this prayer (of all the prayers in the Bible) matter so much?

COME WITH ME TO STUTTGART, Germany, in the last terrible days of World War II. Before us is the famous Church of the Hospitallers. The pastor is a noted young theologian named Helmut Thielicke. Bombs fall day and night as the final German resistance crumbles. Slowly, relentlessly, the mighty Russian army approaches from the east. In the west the Allies gain more ground every day. It is only a matter of days until the "thousand year" Reich falls to the ground.

Through the long years of the war, Pastor Helmut Thielicke preached the gospel to his congregation. Now the end is in sight. What will he say to his people amid the carnage, the death, the destruction, the killing, the gore, the violence, the collapse of society, the fall of Hitler, and the Allied occupation? What does a man say in a moment like that? Where does he go to find the truth his people need to hear? The pastor preached a series of sermons that became so famous they were put in a book (later translated into English and published in America). The sermon series he preached as the war drew to its tragic climax was based on the Lord's Prayer.[1]

I don't know how that strikes you, but it seems unusual to me. Odd. Esoteric. When the bombs are falling on every hand, why would a man talk about something theoretical like the Lord's Prayer? Why wouldn't he talk about something practical? I do not mean that as some sort of critical comment, for I, too, am a pastor, and week by week I must bring the Word of the Living God to my own people. And certainly I have never been in that sort of situation. But very few pastors would decide to preach on the Lord's Prayer when the world is falling apart. Should that not be reserved for a more tranquil time?

Looking back on his experience, Thielicke commented that he could see the fear and desperation on the faces of his hearers. They lived in constant tension, not knowing when the Allied planes would return, bringing with them more bombs, more destruction, still more death, and the end of the world they had built and believed in, even when they didn't accept every part of it. He spoke of the "torment of doubt and despair" of the people as they reached out for hope.

> All that the preacher read in those faces and also what filled him to the brim, since he too was a participant, is doubtless reflected in these sermons. And the Lord's Prayer was able to contain it all. There was not a single question that we could not have brought to it and not a one that would have been suddenly transformed if it were put in the form of a prayer.[2]

I was greatly struck by one sentence, "The Lord's Prayer was able to contain it all."

A PRAYER FOR ALL SEASONS

That one sentence, rightly understood, is the reason I wrote this book. In twenty centuries of Christian history, no prayer has surpassed the eloquent simplicity of the Lord's Prayer. There aren't many things that unite Christians of all persuasions, but the Lord's Prayer is one of them. I don't know how old I was when I first learned the Lord's Prayer, but I couldn't have been more than four or five or six years old. I feel like I've known it all my life. My travels in recent years have taken me around the world and into churches that span the denominational spectrum. I have shared in a Russian Orthodox worship service and clapped my hands with a happy group of Haitian believers. At this moment I pastor an interdenominational church in a Chicago suburb. Each Sunday people from forty to fifty different denominations worship with us. I have discovered that all

Christians know the Lord's Prayer. It transcends language and ritual and culture and race. Simple though it is—and perhaps because of its simplicity—the Lord's Prayer is part of the glue that holds the body of Christ together. We love to argue about doctrine and to debate which church is right, but in the end when we begin to say "Our Father in heaven," our hearts join as one to repeat these ancient words that speak with such contemporary power.

Several years ago I was chagrined to discover that the Lord's Prayer is considered one of the three foundational documents of the Christian faith. To be more accurate, I was chagrined to discover that I didn't know that. Evidently I was absent the day they mentioned the three foundational documents in my church history class at seminary.

If you go back through church history five hundred or one thousand or even fifteen hundred years, you discover that the Lord's Prayer is mentioned in every catechism of the Christian church. That's a crucial fact, because throughout history the catechisms, which are basically Christian doctrine taught in question-and-answer fashion, were used to teach people who couldn't read the doctrines of the Christian faith. That's how Christianity spread in the generations before the printing press revolutionized the world.

All the major catechisms of the Christian faith include the Lord's Prayer as one of the three foundational documents. The other two foundational documents are the Apostles' Creed and the Ten Commandments. The Apostles' Creed tells us what we believe. The Ten Commandments tell how we are to behave. The

Lord's Prayer teaches us how we are to pray. Think of it as belief, action, and prayer. It's all right there. As you go back into church history and look at all branches of the Christian church—Orthodox, Catholic, and Protestant—wherever you find a catechism, you will always find a section about the Lord's Prayer.

A PRAYER FOR THE WORLD

During my first visit to Russia shortly before the collapse of Communism, our team visited eight churches; in six of the eight churches, the choir sang the Lord's Prayer as part of the worship service. It happened in country churches, city churches, big churches, small churches, and in churches by the Volga River. It was a standard part of the service in Russia. But the same is true in churches around the world. The Lord's Prayer is not something small or peripheral. It's central to our understanding of what the Christian faith is all about.

As I write these words, I have completed my twenty-third year as an ordained pastor. As I consider my congregation, I cannot think of anything that we need more than to come into a deeper knowledge of our Lord through prayer. I have no greater burden than for my church truly to become a praying church and for us truly to become people of prayer. We pray in bits and pieces and spasmodically and sporadically, but my heart longs to see us become true people of prayer.

It is clear to me that our real needs aren't financial. Whatever problems we have aren't related to our buildings or our programs. And we don't have many theological problems. The real challenge before us is the challenge of prayer—to know Jesus

Christ better and to bring our needs to him in a deeper and more personal and more intimate way.

What I say about my own church is not unique. Almost every pastor would say the same thing. We all need to pray, we want to pray, we feel the call to pray, and we dream of a church that can truly be called a "praying church." It occurs to me that it is hard to define exactly what the term means, but you know it when you see it. Or sense it. Or feel it.

And that brings us back to the Lord's Prayer as a foundational document. When the disciples wanted to know how to pray, Jesus taught them this simple prayer. We can always do more once we have prayed the Lord's Prayer, but we can hardly say we have prayed at all until we have prayed as Jesus taught us to pray. For many of us our problem may be stated simply: We have heard the Lord's Prayer so many times that by now we take it for granted.

Martin Luther said that the Lord's Prayer was "the greatest Martyr" because "everyone tortures and abuses it." He meant that in his day when people went to church—morning, noon, or night—they always recited or sang the Lord's Prayer. They did it so often that it became a meaningless habit. You could say it by memory without even thinking about it. It's easy to see how that could happen.

We know it too well. We understand it too little. So I'm going to ask you for a personal favor. As you read these chapters, open your mind and your heart with me as we go back to the greatest of all Christian prayers.

At this point I should mention two objections that are sometimes raised against an emphasis on the Lord's Prayer. Some people have suggested that the Lord's Prayer is not really a Christian prayer since it occurs in the Sermon on the Mount and that means (according to certain interpreters) that it is not a description of Christian discipleship. The simplest answer is to observe that this prayer has been almost universally received as a prayer for believers today. Beyond that, we can simply add that there is nothing in this prayer that is not taught elsewhere in the New Testament. If Christ taught us to pray this way, how could it not be a Christian prayer?

And some people object to calling this "the Lord's Prayer." They say that John 17 should be "the Lord's Prayer." This prayer should be called "the Disciples' Prayer." I won't quibble over titles since the New Testament never calls this "the Lord's Prayer." That's simply the title handed down by church history. Some even point out that Jesus, the sinless Son of God, would never pray, "Forgive us our debts." True, but on the cross he prayed, "Father, forgive them, because they do not know what they are doing" (Luke 23:34 HCSB). In any case, this is the prayer our Lord taught us to pray, which means it is truly "the Lord's Prayer" since he is its author.

TWO BEGINNING OBSERVATIONS

Let's begin with two simple observations. *First, the Lord's Prayer is given to us as a guide, a pattern, a model, or a framework for what Christian prayer is all about.* When we think about the Lord's Prayer, we tend to go to one of two extremes. One extreme is to demand that whenever you have a church service, you must recite the Lord's Prayer. Certainly there is nothing wrong or unbiblical with that practice. The other extreme is never to use it in public or private worship. Surely this is an overreaction. The way of wisdom is somewhere between those two extremes. There is no biblical mandate to say the Lord's Prayer every Sunday, but we would do well to have a greater grasp of what Jesus was saying when he gave us this prayer.

The Lord's Prayer is a model, a pattern, or a framework. It is the answer to the question: what does Christian prayer look like? Christian prayer looks like the Lord's Prayer. It doesn't have to sound like the Lord's Prayer. It can be said in different languages. It certainly will be said in different words and in different forms and styles. But truly Christian prayer looks like the Lord's Prayer. It is given as a pattern to teach us what prayer is all about.

Second, the Lord's Prayer is mentioned twice in the New Testament—once in Matthew 6 and once in Luke 11. The version in Matthew 6 is a little bit longer and is considered the traditional version of the Lord's Prayer.

A SIMPLE PRAYER

With that as background, we pick up the story in Matthew 6, the middle chapter of the Sermon on the Mount. In this section Jesus is talking with his disciples about true and false giving, true and false praying, and true and false fasting. When Jesus got to the subject of prayer, he said there is a false kind of prayer, which is praying to be heard, and there is a true kind of prayer, which is going into your prayer closet and praying to your Father in secret from your heart. Then he gives us the Lord's Prayer in Matthew 6:9–13, *"This, then, is how you should pray: Our Father in heaven, hallowed be your name, your kingdom come, your will be done on earth as it is in heaven. Give us today our daily bread. Forgive us our debts, as we also have forgiven our debtors. And lead us not into temptation, but deliver us from the evil one. For yours is the kingdom and the power and the glory forever. Amen."*

As we stand back and look at the prayer as a whole, three things come quickly to mind:

First, how simple this prayer is. No long words, no strange theological expressions, no obscure phrases, no genealogies. The simplicity explains why Christians for two thousand years have gravitated toward it.

Second, how brief it is. Too many long-winded Christians think because of their many words they'll be heard by God. The Lord's Prayer contains only sixty-five words. In the Greek no petition has more than ten words. It's hard to be briefer (or simpler) than "your kingdom come" or "your will be done." Short and to the point. What a great lesson for us.

Third, how comprehensive it is. Everything you'd ever want to say in prayer is in here. Everything. It's in here somewhere—all in this prayer.

THE PRAYER THAT HAS IT ALL

God is in this prayer. We are in this prayer. The past is in this prayer. The present is in this prayer. The future is in this prayer. Father, Son, and Holy Spirit are in this prayer. Everything is here.

Let me share a simple outline for the Lord's Prayer. The first half of the prayer talks about God—*his* name, *his* kingdom, *his* will. The second half of this prayer talks about man—give *us*, forgive *us*, lead *us*. So God and man form the two great subjects of this prayer.

Look now at the second half of the prayer. You'll find the *past*—forgive us our debts, the *present*—give us today, and the *future*—lead us not into temptation. Notice the trinitarian structure in both halves of the prayer:

- Hallowed be your name—the Father magnifies his name.
- Your kingdom come—the Son establishes his kingdom.
- Your will be done—the Holy Spirit executes the will of God.
- Give us today our daily bread—the Father's provision.
- Forgive us our debts—the Son's pardon from sin.
- Lead us not into temptation—the Holy Spirit's protection from temptation.

PRAYER BEGINS WITH GOD

Jesus taught us to say, "Our Father in heaven." Then we talk to the Father about the Father. Prayer begins with God. It doesn't begin with us. Focusing upward, we talk to the Father about his name, his kingdom, and his will. Then we talk to the Father about his family. We pray for provision: "Give us today our daily bread." We pray for pardon: "Forgive us our debts." We pray for protection: "Lead us not into temptation." So we begin with God and move to our own needs. We talk to the Father about the Father, and then we talk to the Father about his family.

Is there anything in heaven or on earth that is not comprehended in those two broad categories? All of life is there. All of eternity is there. All that was and is and is to come is there. If there is something you want to pray about that isn't in those two categories, perhaps it is not worthy of your time or God's attention. Everything that is legitimate content for prayer can be found in the Lord's Prayer. This must be what Pastor Thielicke meant when he said, "The Lord's Prayer was able to contain it all."

HE KNOWS WHAT WE NEED

Before we jump into the prayer itself, let's take a moment to consider a question that has troubled many people: "If God is sovereign, why pray?" I would suppose that most Christians have wondered about it at one time or another. Certainly skeptics have thrown it in our faces to discourage us from seeking the Lord in times of crisis. I would be less than honest if I didn't say that I myself have wrestled with this issue on more than one occasion. Here are five concepts that help us put this question in the proper perspective:[3]

1. *God knows all things.* We call this aspect of God's character his omniscience. It speaks to the fact that because God is God, he knows all things that could be known—past, present, and future—and he knows them at the same time. That means that God is never surprised and that he never learns anything new.

2. *God has committed himself to provide for his people.* We can state it even more forcefully than that. God *wants* to provide for us, he *intends* to provide for us, and he *will* provide what we need. In Philippians 4:19, Paul assures us that "God will supply all your needs" (HCSB), which is the New Testament version of Psalm 23:1, "The LORD is my shepherd, I shall not be in want." David also said in Psalm 34:9, "Fear the LORD, you his saints, for those who fear him lack nothing." God promises, "I will refresh the weary and satisfy the faint" (Jer. 31:25). When we pray, "Give us today our daily bread," do we not pray to a God who has promised to give us all the bread we need precisely when we need it? The whole record of the Bible teaches us that God is the Great Provider, which is why one of his divine names is Jehovah Jireh, "the LORD will provide" (Gen. 22:14).

3. *God has invited us to bring our needs to him.* We are told to ask, to seek, and to knock (Matt. 7:7–8). Why? Ask and it shall be given, seek and you will find, knock and the door will be opened unto you. In Psalm 81:10, the Lord declares, "Open wide your mouth and I will fill it." This is where prayer becomes intensely personal. Our Heavenly Father—who already knows our needs—invites us to make our needs known through prayer.

4. *We don't know what we really need.* We think we do, but we don't. Or to be more accurate, we know part of our needs but not all of them. Our perspective is inevitably limited by our own experience, desires, and personal knowledge. Romans 8:26 reminds us that "we do not know what to pray for" (HCSB). How true that is! Recently I was presented with a problem involving a couple whose marriage has been in crisis for many

years. I can honestly say that I have prayed so much for this couple without a positive result that now when I try to pray, I don't know how to pray for them effectively. That's why the most basic prayer is always "Your will be done." But God knew that we would often be baffled in prayer, so he sent the Holy Spirit who intercedes for us. He prays for us when we don't know how to pray for ourselves or for anyone else.

5. *God knows what we need before we ask him.* Matthew 6:8 says this very plainly: "Your Father knows the things you need before you ask Him" (HCSB). That means we don't have to impress God, or use big words, or pray long prayers. We don't have to repeat ourselves when we pray, and we don't have to worry about getting all the details correct or throw in flowery language when we pray. Since God knows us through and through, he knows our needs better than we do. When you pray, you aren't informing God of anything. He knew your need before you bowed your head.

But that brings us back to the original question. If God knows everything before we pray, and if he truly wants to provide for us anyway, why bother praying at all? Isn't prayer just a waste of time? Or you might say it this way: If God has ordained all things, won't he do whatever he's going to do, with or without my prayers? The answer goes something like this: *We do not pray to inform God of anything.* Because God knows all things from the beginning to the end, he knows the future as well as he knows the past. It is not as if God "needs" our prayers in order to gather accurate information. God doesn't need our prayers, but we need to pray. We pray in order to express our complete dependence on our Heavenly Father. We pray to build our faith. We pray because he is God and we are not. We pray because God has ordained that our prayers are part of his unfolding plan for the universe. In that sense there is no contradiction between God's sovereignty and our prayers.

God invites us to join with him in the great adventure of advancing the cause of Christ in the world. We "partner" with God when we pray. You might even say that God voluntarily "limits" what he does in the world so that we can join with him in prayer. That's why we can truly say that some things happen when we pray that wouldn't happen otherwise if we didn't pray. That's a truly awesome thought. Billy Graham comments that there are rooms in heaven filled with answers to questions that no one on earth has thought to ask. I think he's right, and that ought to motivate us to pray fervently to the Lord.

Picture a father watching his four-year-old daughter trying to put together a puzzle. She tries and tries, but she just can't get the pieces in the right place. Her father watches with great interest, but he doesn't interfere. Finally, she crawls in his lap and says, "Daddy, would you help me put my puzzle together?" He smiles and bends down, and together they begin to pick up each piece. One by one they put the puzzle together.

Why didn't the father help his daughter earlier? For one thing, she didn't ask for his help. For another, he wanted her to try on her own. And most of all, he wanted her to ask for his help. When she did, he was honored and gladly helped her finish the puzzle.

Is this not a picture of how our Heavenly Father deals with his children? Although he longs to come to our aid, often he waits until we ask him specifically. Sometimes he wants us to come to the end of our own pitiful resources before he intervenes. When we cry out in despair, he is honored as we express our complete dependence upon him.

Every prayer is the cry of a child saying, "Help, Father. I can't do this by myself."

PRAYING FOR THE LOST

I've already said that since God knows what we need before we ask him, we don't have to repeat ourselves to get his attention. But that's not the whole story. We all know from personal experience that not all our prayers are answered the first time we pray them. Sometimes we receive immediate answers, but often we must wait days, week, months, or even years before the answer comes.[4] How long should you pray for your loved ones to be saved? My answer is simple. You should pray until God answers your prayers.

Do you remember the story of the widow and the unjust judge in Luke 18:1–8? The woman kept coming back to the judge to plead her case. Because the judge was dishonest, he didn't have time for her, but her persistence wore him down, so finally he said, "I will give her justice, so she doesn't wear me out by her persistent coming" (HCSB). Listen to the words of Jesus as he applies this story to our Heavenly Father: "Will not God grant justice to His elect who cry out to Him day and night? Will

He delay to help them? I tell you that He will swiftly grant them justice" (Luke 18:7–8 HCSB).

Jesus isn't saying that God is like the unjust judge. But if an unjust judge can be swayed by the persistence of a widow, won't God's heart be moved by the persistent prayers of his people? The answer is yes. Persistent prayer moves the heart of God because it expresses such desperate dependence on him. Sometimes it takes desperate circumstances to bring forth this kind of faith. Perhaps you've heard about the doctor who said to his patient, "There's nothing I can do. It's in the hands of God now." "Oh no," the patient replied, "has it come to that?" Prayer reminds us that in the end everything depends on God and not on us.

James 5 gives us another wonderful example of the power of prayer. Elijah prayed that it would not rain, and for three and a half years there was no rain in Israel. He prayed again, and the rains fell from heaven. Here's the moral of the story: "The effective, fervent prayer of a righteous man avails much" (James 5:16 NKJV). *Fervent prayers get God's attention because they come from a heart that believes God's power is unlimited.* This doesn't mean that you need to shout when you pray or that you have to weep or moan or stand or sit. Fervent prayer is simply prayer offered in earnest petition to God. It's not the words that matter or the length of the prayer or the tone of your voice or whether you stand or kneel or sit. What matters is that you really mean what you pray.

Many years ago I heard a noted Christian leader speak at a youth workers' rally in Long Beach. He told how his wife had been involved in a terrible accident. As the ambulance rushed her to the hospital, he tried to pray, but the only words that would come out were, "Oh God! Oh God! Oh God!" It seemed, he commented, like one of the few times in his life that he had entered into the true spirit of prayer.

The same thing happened to me the night our first child was born. My wife had carried the baby for ten full months, and there were some difficulties at the end of the pregnancy. She was in labor all night long, but nothing seemed to be happening. Finally the doctor came in about 5:30 A.M. and said, "We're going to take that baby *now.*" I knew from the look on his face that he felt things weren't going well. Moments later they whisked my wife away, and I was left alone. I tried to pray, but the words wouldn't come. The only prayer that passed my lips was, "Oh God, have mercy. O Lord, have mercy."

I learned that night that prayer is less a matter of using specific words and more a matter of the heart. Fervent prayers move God to action because they come from persistent faith in the face of desperate circumstances. I also learned that the more something means to you, the harder praying for it becomes. The reason we can pray so easily for others is that we're not that deeply invested in them. It's relatively easy to say a brief prayer for people in Thailand or Botswana or Latvia. After all, you don't know them personally, and you'll probably never meet them. You don't have any personal investment in them. It is much different when you try to pray for those who are closest to you. The more you care, the harder it is to pray. When it comes to those things in life that really matter—your husband, your wife, your children, your loved ones—those things are hard to pray for because they are close to your heart.

THE FIRST RULE OF THE SPIRITUAL LIFE

A few years ago I came face to face with a truth I call The First Rule of the Spiritual Life: *He's God, and we're not.* All prayer is based on this simple truth. He runs the universe; we don't. We pray because he's in charge and we're not. And here's a crucial insight: When we don't pray, it's because we've forgotten who's God and who's not. A lack of prayer means we're still trying to run the show. It's a sign that we've decided we can handle things on our own. Sometimes you see little signs that say, "Prayer changes things." I believe that's true. And the first thing prayer changes is us. It teaches us to depend completely on our Heavenly Father, and it reminds us that he is God and we are not.

Why pray if God knows everything in advance? Because God has ordained that our prayers are part of his plan for the universe. Our prayers really do matter to God. In a sense God limits what he can do in the world so that he can work through our prayers. It's not that God "needs" our prayers. He doesn't. But in his grace he has invited us to join him in the great adventure of bringing his kingdom to this sinful world. Through our prayers we partner with God in changing the world. Our greatest problem is not with God's sovereignty but with our own sinful unbelief. The Bible says, "Ye have not, because ye ask not" (James 4:2 KJV). But Jesus himself invited us to ask God for anything that we need. So why don't we pray more than we do?

Let's wrap up this chapter with a very simple theology of prayer. *Our part is to pray fervently, sincerely, and honestly, bringing our deepest concerns to the Lord. God's part is to listen to our prayers and graciously to answer them in his own time, in his own way, according to his own will.* If we do our part, God cannot fail to do his. In that spirit we approach the Lord's Prayer with humility, saying with the first disciples, "Lord, teach us to pray." Through prayer we journey from wherever we are on earth to the very heart of God. The Father invites us to come into his throne room any time and all the time. The King of Kings wants to hear from you. Don't keep him waiting any longer.

A TRUTH TO REMEMBER: ***Everything that is legitimate to pray about can be found in the Lord's Prayer.***

GOING DEEPER

1. What did Pastor Thielicke mean when he said, "The Lord's Prayer was able to contain it all"?

2. Take a moment to think through the various parts of the Lord's Prayer. Which part is most personally significant to you right now? Why?

3. Do you believe the Lord's Prayer should be a regular part of every public worship service? Why or why not?

4. How would you answer the question, If God is sovereign, why pray?

PRAYER

Lord Jesus,

We say with the disciples, "Teach us to pray."

Give us hearts that truly want to pray. Without you we can do nothing. Even our prayers are ineffective without your help.

May our study of the Lord's Prayer be more than an intellectual exercise.

Set our hearts afire with a fresh desire to know you.

Amen.

5. What would a church devoted to prayer look like? What impact would it have on its community? How would you rate the prayer life of your own congregation?

Finish this sentence: "The one thing that keeps me from growing deeper in prayer is ____________."

AN ACTION STEP

Rewrite the Lord's Prayer, putting it into your own words. Add any phrases that help you express each petition in terms of your own circumstances. Try praying your version of the Lord's Prayer for seven days. Feel free to revise the wording as you discover new ways to express this ancient prayer in a personal way.

"Our Father in heaven."
MATTHEW 6:9

CHAPTER TWO
GOD OUR FATHER

Before we begin: What words describe your earthly father? Do you feel comfortable addressing God as "Father"? Why or why not?

THE INTERVIEWER LOOKED AT ME and asked expectantly, "Who is God?" I fumbled to find an answer. Since the cameras were rolling, I had to say something, so I more or less said what I learned in seminary many years ago: "God is an infinite, personal, eternal Spirit who created the universe by his own power. He is all-knowing, all-powerful, and present everywhere at all times. And he exists eternally as Father, Son, and Holy Spirit." As I look back on that definition, I like the first two words: "God is." Everything after that, while very true, sounds like a recitation from a theology lecture.

A few years ago E. V. Hill preached at a Promise Keepers rally in Chicago on those two words: "God is." In his own unforgettable style, he pressed home the point that everything in the universe flows from this one truth. Hill would preach for a while, and then he would say, "God is." He'd preach a while longer, and then he'd say (or whisper or shout), "God is."

He's right, of course. Figure this out, and you've got a handle on life. Deny this, and nothing else makes sense. Either God is, or he isn't. And if he is, that changes everything. The voice from the burning bush told Moses to tell the people that "I AM" had sent him to them (Exod. 3:14). And what precisely does that mean? The only further explanation is "I AM who I AM," which points to God's eternal self-existence. If you know that "God is" and that he is the great "I AM," you know the most fundamental truth in the universe.

WHEN YOU NEED TO KNOW

Not long ago a young couple came to see me with the good news that they plan to be missionaries. They are eminently qualified and will do a wonderful job, and there was only one small problem. After months of prayer they had no idea where they would like to go. "You mean in the whole wide world you have no idea where God wants you to go?" I asked. They didn't have a clue. And they can't start raising support until they at least know where they are going.

As we talked, I said something like this: "The reason you don't know now is because you don't need to know now. If you needed to know now, God would show you. Since you don't know now, it must be true that you don't need to know. Because when you do need to know, you'll know, and not one minute sooner. If God is God, that must be true." I more or less made that up on the spot, but looking back I decided that it was good advice because it is based on the truth that God gives us guidance when we need it, and generally that guidance comes just in the nick of time.

When I shared that with my congregation, people chuckled because it sounds humorous. The key phrase is: "If God is God, this must be true."

A few months later that same couple came to see me with the news that through a very unusual set of circumstances (it always seems to happen this way), God opened the door for them to go to Russia to work in a theological school not far from the Black Sea. When I talked to them earlier, they had no idea such a place existed, much less that they would be going there. But now God has answered clearly, and they are preparing to leave soon for the mission field.

In Psalm 81:10, God gives a wonderful invitation to his children, "Open wide your mouth and I will fill it." Ask what you need, God says, and I will do it for you. Years ago I heard someone say that Jeremiah 33:3 is "God's telephone number" because it contains a very clear promise: "Call to Me, and I will answer you, and I will tell you great and mighty things, which you do not know" (NASB).

WE DO NOT PRAY ALONE

The Lord's Prayer begins with a simple statement about who God is. Jesus invites us to say "Our Father" when we pray. *The key to understanding the Lord's Prayer is rightly understanding what that phrase means.* First of all, when you say, "*Our* Father in heaven," you are admitting that you do not pray alone. The Lord's Prayer is not a "private" prayer. The words *I* and *me* are nowhere to be found. You are admitting that you are not the only one in the world who has a concern to bring to God.

To begin with the word *our* means that you are in a fellowship and a community of God's children around the world. This is an important insight because it is easy to become me-oriented when we pray. But when you pray "Our Father," you are confessing that your problems are not the only problems in the world. You are admitting that there are millions of people around the world who have concerns just as great as yours. To pray like this imparts a bigness and expansiveness to your prayer because it includes all of God's children everywhere.

When we pray "Our Father" as a congregation, we cease to be individuals coming to church with our own particular burdens. Instead, we become part of a family with a common heritage and with shared values. And that family of brothers and sisters is even more decisive than a biological family. It is a family created by the new birth and made possible by the shedding of the blood of Jesus Christ for our redemption.[1]

And that leads us to a crucial theological point. The first step in prayer is to learn to call God "Father." In a true biblical sense, the only people who can do that are those who are the children of God through faith in Jesus Christ (Gal. 3:26). It is popular today to say, "We're all God's children," with a kind of glibness that blurs the distinctions between those who know Jesus Christ and those who don't. In contrast to those who would apply the Lord's Prayer to everyone, even to non-Christians, we must declare that this is a prayer only true Christians can pray. That is, this is not a prayer for Buddhists or Hindus or Muslims. They have their own prayers and their own rituals based on their beliefs. Those prayers belong to them, not to those who claim to follow Jesus Christ. And the same is true of the Lord's Prayer. It is a uniquely Christian prayer based on Christian truth, and it is intended for those who have been born into God's family through faith in Jesus Christ.[2] Charles Haddon Spurgeon notes that it is not a general prayer intended for the masses but is instead a prayer for the true disciples of Christ, those who have been converted by the saving grace of God.[3]

LIKE FATHER, LIKE SON

You are to call him "Our Father." When you call God "Father," you are saying there is One in heaven who hears, knows, understands, cares. Whatever a good father on earth would do for his children, that's what God in heaven will do for his children. The Greek word is *abba,* which means something like "Dearest Father." It's a tender word that speaks of the intimate relationship that exists between a father and his children.

As I write those words, my mind drifts to my own father who died more than a quarter of a century ago. He was a busy surgeon who went to the hospital early in the morning and didn't come home until late at night. I smile when I recall that if he found me doing my homework when he came home, he would give me a quarter. I think I earned about seventy-five cents that way. From him I inherited my love of the Ole Miss Rebels, my Southern accent, and most of the values I hold deep in my heart. It occurred to me recently that I had forgotten how my father's voice sounded. We don't have any tape recordings of his voice, so it's been a long time since I heard it. As I pondered the matter, I realized with a kind of inner certainty that if my father were to enter a crowded room and say just one word, "Son," I would know it was him, would know it instantly, would know it without even seeing his face. Though my father is gone, he is not forgotten, for he lives on in me and through me.

I now have three sons of my own, and they know without my having to tell them that because I am their father, I am always glad to see them. A few years ago, while presiding at a late-night prayer meeting, this truth came home to me in a powerful way. It must have been about 9:45 P.M., and I was offering some words of instruction to the people gathered in the room. While I was speaking to the group, one of my boys walked up to me to ask me a question. I paused, listened to him, answered him, and then continued with my talk. When we had a break a few minutes later, one of the men commented on what my son had done. I didn't even remember it. The whole episode happened so naturally that it didn't register in my memory. My son knew he could talk to me any time he wanted, and that's what he did.

Sons and daughters have family rights that guarantee them access to their father. That's a big part of what being a father is all about. My children don't need an appointment to see me, and I don't need an appointment to see my Heavenly Father. Even in the midst of running the entire universe, keeping the stars in their courses, and making sure the planets don't run into one another, and while he oversees six billion people with all their troubles, cares, worries, fears, problems, and difficulties, our God still has time for us. He listens to us as if he had nothing else to do.

A FRIEND IN HIGH PLACES

We pray to our Father who is "in heaven." That's usually a throwaway line for most of us. We tend to think it means that earth is where we are and heaven is where God is, which we imagine is beyond the farthest star. That's not what it means. The phrase "in heaven" refers to heaven as the center of the universe and the seat of all authority, power, dominion, and greatness. You are on earth and are therefore limited to this little ball of dirt floating around the sun in a little corner of a big galaxy called the Milky Way. And that galaxy is just one of millions of galaxies in a universe so huge that we cannot accurately measure it. To say that we are "on earth" means that we pray from a position of weakness and comparative insignificance. God is in the seat of all authority and all power. Therefore, when you say, "Our father in heaven," you are proclaiming that he has the authority and power to hear you and to help you when you pray. It is precisely because God is in heaven that he has the power to help you.

Think of it this way:

- "*Our* Father" speaks of community.
- "Our *Father*" speaks of family.
- "*In heaven*" speaks of authority.

Or to say it another way:

- Our = I do not pray alone.
- Father = I am not left alone.
- In heaven = I do not struggle alone.

Or from a third perspective:

- Our = I pray with others.
- Our Father = I pray to One who cares for me.
- Our Father in heaven = I pray to One who has the power to help me.

Every single word is important. Every single word is crucial. *Our* opens you up to a big view of the universe. *Father* encourages you to believe that he cares. *In heaven* means that you don't have a problem that he can't handle. You don't have a need in your life that he can't meet because he's a father in heaven who hears and answers prayer.

A NEW WAY OF LOOKING AT GOD

Without a doubt the central word is *Father.* A quick glance at a concordance reveals that the name "Father" is applied to God infrequently in the Old Testament and never by a person referring to God as "my Father." It always refers to God as the Father of the nation of Israel. When we come to the New Testament, we discover that Jesus called God "Father" more than sixty times.[4] Why this enormous difference? Because the revelation of God as our personal Father is based on the coming of Jesus Christ into the world. It's not that he wasn't a Father to his people in the Old Testament, but that's not the primary way he revealed himself. Only in the New Testament do we discover that God is now the Father of those who come to the Lord Jesus Christ by faith.

The word *Father* in the Bible means three basic things. First, it refers to source or paternity or origin. God is the source of all that you have. When we sing the doxology, we begin with the words "Praise God from whom all blessings flow." Or as the Scripture says, "For in Him we live and move and exist" (Acts 17:28 HCSB). When you call God "Father," you declare that your ultimate origin rests with him.

Second, the word *Father* speaks of parental authority. He is God, and you are not. He is running the show, and you are not. He is a father; you are his child. We must not use the fact of God's love as an excuse to reject his right to rule over us. Because he is our Father "in heaven," he has the right to do as he pleases even if his ways do not always make sense to us. "He may send us pain and circumstances that frustrate us. We must not act like spoiled children when this occurs."[5] We should affirm our confidence in his goodness toward us at all times.

Third, when you call God "Father," you confess that he is a God of tender, loving care. A Hebrew word in the Old Testament, *hesed,* is translated a number of different ways. In the King James *hesed* is usually translated as lovingkindness. As in "thy lovingkindness is better than life." The newer translations take that concept and add the concept of faithfulness to it. This word speaks of God's loyal love to all his children. It is the love that keeps on loving no matter what we do or how badly we blow it or how many dumb mistakes we make. He is a God who never lets his children go. He loves his children with an everlasting love that is faithful and loyal no matter what happens.

When we were far away, he loved us. When we turned our back on him, he loved us. When we broke his law, he loved us. When we went our own way, he loved us. When we said, "Leave us alone, we don't want you around anymore," he said, "I'm going to stay around anyway." And when we ran, he followed. When we hid, he found us. When we cursed him to his face, he just smiled and said, "I love you anyway." That's what loyal love is all about. That's the Father's love for his children. He is always near us whether we see him or feel him or even when we doubt he is there.

He calms our fears.

He cheers us on.

He provides what we really need.

He lets us go our own way.

He welcomes us back from the far country.

GOOD NEWS FOR PRODIGAL SONS AND DAUGHTERS

Jesus told a story that beautifully illustrates this truth (Luke 15:11–32). We call it the parable of the prodigal son. It's all about a young man who made a foolish decision and what happened to him as a result. The story begins with a younger son who chafes under his father's rule and perhaps feels put down by his obedient older brother. So he demands his inheritance from his father, who agrees to give it to him. Taking the money, he leaves home and journeys to a place the Bible calls "a far country." There he spends every dime he has on riotous living. Parties day and night, women on both arms, the good life, the fast lane. Whatever he wants, he buys with his father's money. Eventually the money runs out. When a famine comes, not having any money and being too far away from home, he attaches himself to a farmer who says, "The only work I have is feeding my pigs." The prodigal son ends up penniless, homeless, starving, feeding the pigs, eating the pods from the carob trees. He who had eaten prime rib just a few weeks earlier now dines with the pigs. *In the end he lost everything.* The prodigal son has hit rock bottom. That's when his life began to change.

First, he came to his senses and realized what a fool he had been. Second, he decided to return to his father. Third, he mentally rehearsed how he would confess his sin to his father. Fourth, he got up from the pigpen and started the long journey home.

As he shuffled along the road, questions went through his mind: *What is my father going to say? Will he take me back?* With his head down he walked along that dirt road, embarrassed and humiliated. Certainly his fears were well founded.

We don't often think about the father's pain when we read this story. But it couldn't have been easy for him. He lost part of the fortune he had worked so long to amass. Then he lost his reputation in the community. When a son leaves home in such anger, there's no way to keep it hidden. The older brother knew, the hired men knew, soon enough the friends and neighbors knew about it. Every time the father went into town, people talked about it behind his back. Dysfunctional families make good gossip for idle minds. They talked about what had happened. They analyzed the problems. Perhaps some of the younger men took the son's side. No doubt the older men sided with the father. Meanwhile, the father knew all about the talk, heard the whispers, and through it all, silently struggled to keep his dignity.

But the worst pain was the simple fact that the father had lost his son. After all those years, after all those prayers, after holding him in his arms, after teaching him how to hunt and fish, after pouring out an ocean of love, suddenly the dream is shattered, and the father is left with a huge hole in his heart. Words cannot express the pain, the sadness, the loss the father feels. His son has left home, and no one can console him.

After all that, could anyone blame the father if he refused to take his son back? No wonder the son worries as he slowly plods toward home. He has no idea what awaits him.

SMOTHERED WITH KISSES

The Bible says that while he was still a long way off, his father saw him. This is a great moment. *His father saw him first.* His father saw him and was moved with compassion. Day after day the father had watched for his son. Night after night he had waited for his return. Nothing deterred him—not the weather, not the jeers and jokes of the skeptics, not the doubting looks of his friends. Deep in his heart he *knew* his son would someday come back home.

Then it happened. One day, late in the afternoon, when the sun was beating down and sweat covered his face, he saw a figure slowly come over the rise and begin to walk hesitantly toward him. Throwing all dignity aside, he ran to meet his son, embraced him, threw his arms around him, and kissed him. The word Jesus used means he smothered him with kisses. In that one moment all questions were answered. The son's fear melted away in the tears and hugs.

No one could ever have predicted what happened next. It is for this that we love this story. We read it over and over. We cling to it, believe it, hope in it, stake out lives upon it—all because of the father's welcome to his erring son.

There are five signs of the father's welcome:

1. The kiss, the sign of forgiveness.
2. The robe, the sign of honor.
3. The ring, the sign of authority.
4. The sandals, the sign of freedom.
5. The feast, the sign of a joyful welcome.

Verse 24 brings the first part of the story to a close with these wonderful words of hope: "So they began to celebrate." At the father's command a party begins that lasts for hours. How does the father feel about his son who has come home? "We had to celebrate and be glad, because this brother of yours was dead and is alive again; he was lost and is found" (Luke 15:32). Back from the dead! Found! Alive again! Home again! No wonder the father said, "Let's have a party." It was the Father's love that made him run to the son while his son was still a great distance away. And that same love caused him to kill the fatted calf and throw an enormous party. The son who was lost had now been found. Even during the darkest days and the longest nights, the father never gave up hope that one day his son would come home. That's what God's "loyal love" is all about.

You've never done anything that could make God stop loving you.

You may say, "But you don't know what I've done this week." That's all right. God knows, and he loves you anyway. You've never even imagined anything that could make God stop loving you.

"I'm far away from God." He still loves you.

"I've sinned." He still loves you.

"You don't understand." I don't have to understand. He knows, and he loves you anyway.

"I don't care. I'm going to go my way." It doesn't matter. He still loves you. And when you're ready, he'll be ready. When you turn around, and you will, he'll be standing at the door to welcome you back.

That's the mighty love of God. That's the love of a God who is called Father. Aren't you glad this prayer didn't begin, "O First Principle, Hallowed be thy name," or "O Ground of all Being, Give us this day our daily bread." We wouldn't have believed that. That wouldn't have helped us.

IS THERE ANYONE UP THERE WHO CARES FOR ME?

The Lord's Prayer answers the greatest questions of the universe: Is there anybody up there who cares about me? Is there anybody up there who watches over me? Is there anybody up there who knows my name? And the answer comes back: Yes. Yes. Yes. *There is a God in heaven who cares about you. And he is called Father.*

This prayer is the answer to the deepest problem of humankind—the problem of fatherlessness. The Lord's Prayer reminds us that if we know Jesus Christ, we are not orphans in the universe. Ever since Adam and Eve sinned in the Garden of Eden, the image of God within each of us has been marred by sin. I picture a piece of paper with the words GOD'S IMAGE in huge letters. Before Adam and Eve sinned, that paper was clean and smooth. Now for all of us that paper is crumpled, dirty, and torn. But it is never completely destroyed. Despite all our failures we still want to know God, and we still want to find meaning in life but just don't know where to look.

FATHER HUNGER

To use a very modern phrase, we are left with a kind of "Father Hunger." That's a phrase used to describe children growing up in a family without a strong and compassionate father figure. He may have died, or he may have abandoned his family. Or perhaps he was so busy that he had no time for his family. Because he barely knows his children, they compete desperately for little scraps of his love and approval. Children growing up in a home like that desperately want a father, and sometimes they will look for someone (or something) to fill that void. On a much larger scale that's the story of all humanity. We were made to know God, and we want to know him, but our sin has separated us from God. As a result we are left with a deep "Father hunger" that won't go away.

Some people become so desperate that they turn to alcohol and drugs to fill the aching void within. Others float from one failed relationship to another. And some people bury themselves in their work in the hope that climbing to the top of the corporate heap will quell the little voice within that says, "There must be something more." In the end a few tortured souls take their own lives because, like Solomon of old, they discovered that nothing in this life satisfies for very long. They end up saying, "I hated life" (Eccles. 2:17).

Good news! Good news! In Jesus Christ we have discovered the greatest news of all—that our God is not some impersonal deity, not fate or chance or some mechanical kismet or karma, not something mystical, not a God who's so far off he doesn't care. In Jesus Christ we've discovered the most important truth of the universe: Our God is a father. He loves you so much that he did something we would never think of doing. He gave his own Son to die for you. He loves you inconceivably because he did the inconceivable. He gave his Son for you, proving that he is a Father who truly loves his children.

All that a good father is to his children God will be to his children when they approach him in prayer. And that is why the most profound prayer you will ever pray has only three words—"Our Heavenly Father." Pray that and if you really understand what it means, that *is* the prayer, and everything else is just the P.S.

Jesus made prayer simple because in the end we are simple people. If it were difficult, most of us would forget it or mess it up somehow. Yet these simple words are profound beyond our understanding. Everything that God has for us and everything he is for us is wrapped up in the word *Father.* When we come to him in Jesus' name, we are not coming to an angry God but to a friendly Father. Don't be afraid to talk to God. Your Father is waiting to hear from you.

GOING DEEPER

1. What do you think of when you hear the word *father*? Are your mental images positive or negative? How does your experience with your earthly father impact your view of God as your Heavenly Father?

2. How have you experienced God's "parental authority" in your life?

3. Read Luke 15:11–32 slowly and thoughtfully. Put yourself in the prodigal son's place. What made him want to leave home? What made him finally decide to come home? How do you think he felt as he prepared to meet his father?

4. Now put yourself in the father's place. Think about the range of emotions he must have felt when his son asked for his share of the estate. How would you have responded in that situation? How did he feel during the long months or years his son was in the "far country"? Why didn't he punish his son when he finally came home? Would you have been tougher than he was?

5. Read Psalm 103:13–18; Matthew 7:7–11; 1 Thessalonians 2:11–12; Hebrews 12:4–11. What do these passages

PRAYER

Lord God,

You have called us out of darkness into your marvelous light, and by grace you have blessed us with every spiritual blessing in Christ.

All things are ours because all things are yours, and we are your beloved children. We claim no merit of our own but cling to the imputed righteousness of your Son, the Lord Jesus Christ.

We make bold to pray the Lord's Prayer because Jesus commanded us to do so, and with his own blood he opened the way into your presence.

We thank you for the privilege of calling you Father.

In Jesus' name.

Amen.

teach us about the characteristics of a good father?

6. What does the term *father hunger* suggest to you? How is your own prayer life strengthened by seeing God as your Father?

A TRUTH TO REMEMBER:
In Jesus Christ we've discovered the most important truth of the universe: Our God is a Father.

AN ACTION STEP

Since God is your Father, he invites you to pour out your heart to him. Take a three-by-five card and jot down three prayer requests that are on your heart right now. At the top write "Ask, Seek, Knock—Matthew 7:7–11." Use this as a simple reminder to bring all your requests before your Heavenly Father.

"Hallowed be your name."
MATTHEW 6:9

CHAPTER THREE
TAKING GOD SERIOUSLY

Before we begin: What does the word *hallowed* mean? What does God's name represent, and why does it matter so much?

LATE ONE WEDNESDAY AFTERNOON my three sons and I had just arrived at a motel in Page, Arizona. Looking out from our picture window, we watched the sun set across the dark blue waters of Lake Powell. It had been a long day of driving that started in Salt Lake City, wound down through Provo, the Big Rock Candy Mountain, Bryce Canyon, and on to a town named Kanab. The next day would find us in Phoenix. But we stopped in Page, checking into our hotel room at 6:47 P.M., just in time to throw our bags in the corner, plop down on the bed, turn on the TV, and watch game five of the

1991 NBA Championship Series between the Chicago Bulls and the Los Angeles Lakers.

Mark and Nicholas went swimming, but Josh and I watched almost the whole game together. It was a close, tight, tense game from beginning to end. Then in the final few minutes John Paxson hit five shots in a row, and the Bulls won the first of their six NBA championships. Pandemonium broke out in the motel room. The boys were celebrating because I promised them that if the Bulls won, we would go out someplace special to eat. We went to a fine restaurant called Taco Bell.

Meanwhile at the Forum in Los Angeles, a vast mob filled the court as the players fought their way to the locker room where they were welcomed with cheers, laughter, and a champagne shower. Then there was a strange sight. Michael Jordan kissed the floor. All the players huddled around him. They were all saying something. It was hard to hear at first. Then the room quieted, and you could hear him clearly: "Our Father, who art in heaven, hallowed be thy name, thy kingdom come, thy will be done, on earth as it is in heaven." And on they went, saying the Lord's Prayer together on national TV.

As I thought about that moment later, it occurred to me that some people might think it sacrilegious to recite the Lord's Prayer after winning a basketball game. I understand the sentiment because we are used to hearing this prayer said in more solemn circumstances. However, there is a sense in which the Lord's Prayer was appropriate for that moment, even more appropriate than if someone had prayed spontaneously. For in praying that prayer at that moment, Michael Jordan and his teammates acknowledged that some things in life are more important than wearing a championship ring.

THE MOST FAMOUS PRAYER IN THE WORLD

As this incident illustrates, the Lord's Prayer is the best-known prayer in the world. No other prayer is known by so many people or said in so many places in so many different languages. Every Sunday in churches around the world—from the mud huts of equatorial Africa to the great cathedrals of Europe, from the white clapboard country churches of rural Mississippi to the house churches of Hong Kong—in literally millions of churches, Christians of every denomination recite this prayer as part of their worship experience. I have already pointed out that the Lord's Prayer is a central document of the Christian faith. For two thousand years believers have pondered its meaning. Like an inexhaustible well, the deeper you go in prayer, the more you find. And no matter how long you study this prayer, the more it reveals to the earnest seeker. Though brief and simple it is also profound—indeed, it is the most profound prayer ever prayed.

CLOISTERED HALLS AND DISMAL CHANTS

Now it's time to look at the first phrase of the first half of the prayer—"Hallowed be your name." I think it's fair to say that this phrase is the one that makes the least sense to us, and therefore it is the phrase we pray the least. Almost all of us will pray, "Give us this day our daily bread," and many of us will pray, "Deliver us from evil." Still others will pray, "Your will be done," and some will even pray, "Your kingdom come." But few of us, if left to ourselves, will ever pray, "Hallowed be your name."

In the first place it simply sounds strange. *Hallowed* is not a word we often use. *Hallowed* is an archaic word that smacks of cloistered halls and dismal chants. When you say "these hallowed halls," you can almost picture a medieval monastery where the old men come strolling through the arches dressed in long brown robes, swinging censers filled with smoky incense, and singing mournful music. That's our basic problem. The phrase itself sounds like it belongs back in the twelfth century. We really don't know what to do with it in the twenty-first century. Our other problem is that we don't know what it means. Since we don't know what it means, we're not really sure what we're praying for. Since we don't know what we're praying for, we tend to skip right over it so we can get down to the part we do understand, like "give us this day our daily bread." Daily bread. Now that's something that makes sense to us.

But it's of paramount importance to note that Jesus didn't begin with the part we understand—like bread and forgiveness. He starts with the part we don't understand. There's a crucial point here. Prayer doesn't begin with our concerns; prayer begins with God's concerns. Or to put it in its simplest form, prayer doesn't begin with us; prayer begins with God.

THIS HALLOWED GROUND

So when we pray to the Father, we are to begin by praying, "Hallowed be your name." Let's look at the word *hallowed.* It's not really that difficult. The word itself means "holy" or "sacred." We sometimes talk about the "hallowed halls of ivy," referring to a great university like Harvard or Yale. Sometimes you hear the phrase "the hallowed halls of Congress," which must be a figure of speech because much that goes on there is not sacred or holy. Then we remember what Abraham Lincoln said in the Gettysburg Address just a few months after the pivotal battle of the Civil War in 1863. Standing on the battlefield where so many men in blue and gray shed their blood, he declared, "We cannot hallow, we cannot consecrate, we cannot dedicate this ground." Why? Because the battlefield at Gettysburg was already hallowed or made sacred by the brave men who fought and died there. That gives us a good definition: To "hallow" something is to treat it as sacred and holy and worthy of the highest veneration and respect.

So the prayer is this: "Lord, may your name be treated with respect and honor because your name is sacred and holy." You hallow God's name when you treat it with the utmost respect.

WHAT'S IN A NAME?

That immediately raises another question. Why did he say, "Hallowed be your *name*"? It's not exactly the same as if we would say, "Hallowed be the name of Frank, or the name of Paul, or the name of Butch, or the name of Ruth, or the name of Sylvia." Your name is important to you. It may not matter to anyone else in the world, but you care about your name because it identifies who you are. Your name may be Sally or Jill or Mary or John or Robert or Phil. You may be one of twenty John Smiths in the phone book, but to you, you are the only John Smith who really matters.

Think of how much time parents spend naming their children. They spend hours thinking about the possibilities—discussing, debating, arguing, writing down a first name, then adding a middle name, then reversing the order or dropping one and adding another.

My full name is Clarence Raymond Pritchard. I was named Clarence for my uncle, who died two years after I was born. Raymond was my father's middle name. When my oldest son was born, we named him Joshua Tyrus Pritchard—Joshua for the great Bible hero and Tyrus in honor of my father, who was named after Ty Cobb, the great baseball player. Our second son was named Mark Alan after my wife's older brother Mark and my younger brother Alan. Then when our third son came along, we named him Nicholas Andrew because . . . well, because we were expecting a girl, and we didn't pick out a boy's name until the very end. We were stuck, so we looked at the roster of Joshua's soccer team, saw a boy named Nicholas, and said, "That sounds good." But the Andrew is in honor of my older brother Andy.

Names mean something. They communicate history, tradition, and family heritage. They identify us with our past, drawing across the generations a shared set of values. In the Bible a name normally stands for the character or the basic attributes of the person who bears the name. For example, *Adam* means "man," and *Eve* means "life giver." *Abraham* means "father of multitudes," and *Jacob* means "cheater." In the New Testament,

Peter means "rock," a reference to Peter's rock-like faith. In Bible times, when you called a person's name, you weren't just identifying him. You were also identifying his character.

We do the same thing today. We all tend to associate certain names with certain emotions. For instance, if I mention Hitler, you instantly think of Nazi Germany and the horrors of the concentration camps. If I mention Mother Teresa, you think of her selfless work for the homeless and dying of Calcutta. Two people. Two names. Two completely different emotions. Or what about, "as honest as Abe Lincoln," or, "He's got the strength of Paul Bunyan." The names mean something. They say something about the character of the person.

What pops up on your mental screen when you hear the word *God*? The answer depends on who you are and how much you know. For most of us, the word *God* brings up images of the stories of the Bible—how God created the world out of nothing, how he parted the Red Sea for the children of Israel, how he caused the walls to come tumbling down at Jericho, how he enabled David's tiny stone to kill Goliath, how he shut the mouths of lions so Daniel could get a good night's sleep.

We know God through the things he has done. We hear the stories, and then we refer to the God who stands behind the stories. God's "name" is his character and his reputation. Let me give you a suggestion for your Bible study. Take your concordance and study how many times the name of God is mentioned in the Bible. You will discover that the Bible mentions the name of God hundreds of times. Consider these few examples:

"O LORD, our Lord, how majestic is *your name in all the earth!*" (Ps. 8:1).

"Some trust in chariots and some in horses, but we trust in *the name* of the LORD our God" (Ps. 20:7).

"He guides me in paths of righteousness for *his name's sake*" (Ps. 23:3).

"For *Your name's sake,* O LORD, Pardon my iniquity, for it is great" (Ps. 25:11 NKJV).

How about this famous verse? "Everyone who calls on the name of the Lord will be saved." That's found three times in the Bible—Joel 2:32, Acts 2:21, and Romans 10:13. God's name represents who he is. It embodies his character. That's why the third commandment says, "You shall not take *the name* of the LORD your God in vain" (Exod. 20:7 NKJV). To take God's name in vain means to take it lightly or flippantly. It's the exact opposite of "hallowing" God's name. Therefore, we might say that to "hallow" God's name means to take it seriously.

WHAT DOES GOD LOOK LIKE?

Now if you pull all that together, this is what "hallowed be your name" really means. "Lord, may your righteous character be seen in the world so that men and women will respect you for who you really are. May your name be made great so that your creatures will give you the honor and respect that is your rightful due."

Or you could say it this way:

"O God, show us who you are."

"O God, may we see you as you are."

"O God, may we treat you as you ought to be treated."

We "hallow" the name of God because he is holy and good. We take it seriously because God's name represents who he is and what he does. We don't take it lightly or flippantly because we don't take God lightly and flippantly. When we pray like this, we are asking God to "cause your word to be *believed,* cause your displeasure to be *feared,* cause your commandments to be *obeyed,* and cause yourself to be *glorified.*"[1]

BACK TO BETHLEHEM

What does God look like? The Bible doesn't leave us to wonder about the answer to that question. Nearly two thousand years ago a little baby was born in Bethlehem who forever answered that question. If you want to know what God is like, look at Jesus. Hebrews 1:3 calls him the "radiance of His glory" (HCSB).

Does God have a name? Yes. His name is Jesus. In him the abstract becomes concrete. When I look at Jesus, all those theoretical ideas about God suddenly become reality.

- God now has hands.
- And feet.
- And eyes to see.
- Ears to hear.
- Lips to speak.
- God has a voice!
- He speaks a language I understand.

I see him touch a leper, and I know no one is too dirty for him.

I see him pause to speak to a beggar, and I know he's never too busy for me.

I see him feed the multitudes with loaves and fishes, and I know he can supply my needs.

I see him with the towel and the basin, and I know no job is too menial for him.

Finally I see him hanging on the cross, suspended between heaven and earth, beaten, bruised, bloodied, mocked, scourged, spat upon, jeered, booed, hated, attacked, scorned, despised, rejected, crucified. When I hear him cry out, "Father, forgive them, because they do not know what they are doing" (Luke 23:34 HCSB), I suddenly understand that Jesus has no enemies. In Jesus I discover a God who takes people seriously. He never treats people casually. He never brushes them off. He never says, "You're a loser." He's a God who cares enough to get involved in this ugly, twisted, unredeemed world.

That's who God is. If he never took people lightly, then I must never take his name lightly.

THE UNHALLOWED NAME

Let me stop here and make one simple observation. No prayer could be more appropriate in a sinful world. For if one thing is certain about the world in the early years of the twenty-first century it is this: God's name is not being hallowed today.

God's name is not hallowed when . . .

- More than a million babies are killed through abortion every year in America.
- Crack cocaine is sold like candy on street corners.
- Homosexuality is celebrated as a natural and normal way of life.
- The divorce rate nearly equals the marriage rate.
- We laugh and giggle at sex on TV when instead we ought to blush.
- God's people think nothing of attending filthy movies.
- We take God's name in vain and laugh at dirty jokes.
- We cheat on our income tax and joke about it.
- We expect our leaders to lie and are surprised when they don't.
- Spiritual leaders fall into sin, and our hearts are not broken.
- Christians keep quiet in order to avoid persecution on the job.
- We secretly envy sinners who do things we are forbidden to do.
- The Bible has become a closed book and prayer a heavy burden.
- We tithe to the mortgage company instead of to the Lord.
- Christian teenagers are encouraged not to consider missionary service.

- We value the approval of others more than the approval of God.
- Social drinking is winked at, and the standards of yesteryear are derided as legalism.
- We gossip about the sins of others instead of mourning over our own sins.
- We criticize our brothers and sisters for failing to live up to our own expectations.
- We hold grudges for days, weeks, months, and even years.

A few years ago a major news organization reported on a survey that compared the ethical behavior of American Christians with the ethical behavior of the general population. The survey reportedly found that there is no substantial difference in the ethical behavior of those who call themselves Christians and the general population. As the world gets more churchy, the church gets more worldly. In such a climate of moral ambivalence, we should not be surprised that the church has become marginalized to the point of irrelevance. True, there is a riding tide of hostility in many quarters today toward anyone who dares to speak out in favor of God and eternal moral values. And in many parts of the world, believers are routinely harassed, arrested, beaten, and sometimes put to death. But in many Western countries, Christians are simply ignored because we look too much like the population at large.

In the early church Christians were thrown to the lions. In too many cases today, we've joined in a limited partnership with the people who own the lions. To say this is not to suggest that we should pray for persecution or that we should adopt some sort of martyr complex. But it is true that if Christians took the name of God more seriously, the people who don't care about God would take us more seriously.

The same is true in the realm of personal relationships. William Barclay points out that if a Christian under pressure loses his temper just like a non-Christian does, or if he becomes just as nervous or anxious, or if he is just as greedy or just as gluttonous or just as cruel or just as materialistic as the man next door . . . that is, if his religion doesn't actually change the way he lives, he shouldn't be surprised that his neighborhood evangelism does not win many converts. After all, why be converted to something that is not much different from what you already have?

> The very essence of this petition is that in it we pray that God may enable us to show that we are redeemed, so that in our lives he may be glorified, and so that through us others may come to desire the secret which we possess. This petition prays that we may be enabled so to show Christ to men that men may desire Christ.[2]

What would we see if we followed you around this week? Would your life show any material difference because you are a Christian? Does the fact that you bear the name of Jesus Christ make a difference in the way you live? That's really the bottom line on this petition.

When you pray, "Hallowed be your name," you are really praying, "O God, help me to live in such a way that your name is made great in my life. May your reputation be increased in the world by the way I live my life."

A few days ago I spoke with a man who nearly lost his oldest daughter in a terrible car accident. "All my life I've heard that God must be number one, then your family must be second, then everything else comes third. When something like this happens, you suddenly learn how true that is," he said.

That's why this request is first. It's fundamental. Before you pray about what you want, you are to pray about what God wants. What God wants is that his name be made great in the world.

WHO IS ON THE THRONE?

Early in my Christian life, a friend gave me a little booklet about the Spirit-filled life. Inside the booklet were three circles with a throne at the center of each circle. In one circle a cross was drawn outside the circle. That represented an unbeliever. Christ is still outside of his life. The next circle showed the cross inside the circle but not on the throne. That represented a Christian who was still running his own life. And the last circle showed the cross inside the circle and above the throne. That represented the believer who had surrendered the throne of his life to Jesus Christ.

I find those three circles helpful and challenging. Each one of us fits one of those three circles. Too many of us live in the middle circle with Christ in our lives but self still on the throne. I confess that too often I am king on my own throne, and my prayers are filled with my own needs. I pray more about myself than I do about God.

Here's a good test for you to take: *If God answered the prayers you prayed today, whose name would be glorified? Yours or his?* But that all changes when you pray, "Hallowed be your name." When you pray it with understanding, you are really saying, "Lord Jesus, ascend to the throne of my life."

A right appreciation of God's name gives us courage in the moment of crisis. Do you remember what David said when he faced Goliath? "You come against me with sword and spear and javelin, but I come against you in the name of the LORD Almighty, the God of the armies of Israel, whom you have defied" (1 Sam. 17:45). Goliath must have laughed when he heard this brash teenager spouting nonsense about the name of the Lord Almighty. Hadn't the Israelites fled in fear for thirty-nine straight days? Hadn't they been afraid to come out and fight? Now here comes this "snot-nosed little runt of a pimple-faced kid" (a description I once heard a speaker give of David) talking trash to the mighty Goliath.

What a joke!

Before the day was over, Goliath discovered the joke was on him. David found a stone, put it in the slingshot, wound up, and let it go. Before Goliath knew what hit him, he fell to the ground. Talk about a lucky shot! Nothing lucky about it. It wasn't the stone that made the difference. It was the courage of David to go into battle "in the name of the Lord."

Somewhere I read the story of a soldier in the army of Alexander the Great who deserted his post in battle. When asked his name, the quaking soldier replied, "Alexander, my Lord." Whereupon Alexander the Great said, "You have three choices. Fight, get out of the army, or change your name." We bear the name of the Lord. His reputation in the world rests on us. We honor that name and increase his reputation when we speak up for him before others. And if we're not going to get into the battle for God, then we ought to get out of the army or change our name.

"COULD GOD SIGN HIS NAME TO THIS?"

In his sermon on this petition, Helmut Thielicke said that you have not learned to pray the Lord's Prayer unless you pray it against yourself.[3] He meant that the Lord's Prayer sets such a high standard that if we really understand what we are praying, we will be praying against our own natural tendencies. Whenever we pray, "Hallowed be your name," we are asking that God's name be made great instead of our own name. But if you really mean that, you are praying "against yourself."

All too often we pray so carelessly. "Hallowed be your name"—

- "But not in my business."
- "But not in my finances."
- "But not in my leisure."
- "But not in my friendships."
- "But not in my sex life."
- "But not in my thought life."
- "But not in my speech."
- "But not in my daydreams."

We say, "Lord, anything but that." And the Lord says, "It's all or nothing." We say, "Lord, I can't hallow your name in this one area of my life. It's too personal, it's too difficult, and it's just the way I am. I'm bitter, angry, upset, worried, greedy, and I can't use your name in this area because that's just the way I am."

We all have areas where we hide things from God because we know he could never sign his name to them. But that's really the acid test for conduct, for questionable things, for bad habits, for angry words, for secret sins, for bad attitudes: "Could God sign his name to this?" When you come to one of those difficult areas of your life, you ought to ask that question: "Could God sign his name to this?" If the answer is yes, then go on with your life. If the answer is no, either stop what you are doing or stop praying the Lord's Prayer. It's really that simple.

RAY TYRUSOVICH

Let's wrap up this chapter with a simple story. On our third or fourth day in Russia I noticed something unusual about the way the men addressed one another. They would say each other's first name, and then they would add a middle name that always ended with *ovich.* My friend John Sergey was addressed as "Ivan Mikhailovich Sergei." When I asked John about it, he said that Russians always use the patronymic. *Patronymic* is a word that means "the name of my father." The *ovich* ending in Russian literally means "son of." Therefore, "Ivan Mikhailovich" literally means "John son of Michael." It's a way of recognizing your family lineage. Every son bears his father's name.

When John asked me my father's name, I told him my dad was named Tyrus Pritchard. His full name was Tyrus Raymond Pritchard. My older brother Andy took his first name, and I took his middle name. John thought for a moment and then said that in Russian my name with the patronymic would be Ray Tyrusovich—"Ray son of Tyrus." That pleased me when I heard it because I've always been proud of my father. The thought of being called by my father's name is one of the greatest honors I could imagine. I think he would be proud and pleased, too.

Even though my father died more than twenty-five years ago, a part of him lives on in me and in my three brothers. If I can be permitted to paraphrase the words of Jesus, if you have seen me, you have seen my father—however imperfectly, however incompletely, however mixed in with other influences on my life. But my dad is there, sure enough, in my face, my voice, my actions, my habits. I even see him in my three sons—fainter still, but the influence is there. My sons are like me in many ways, but I am like my father in some ways, and so his influence passes on to the third generation.

Sometimes when I visit my relatives, one of them will say, "You remind me so much of your father." I could receive no finer compliment. That's what it means to bear my father's name. It is far more than having the same last name. His character and personality were in some small way passed on to me. And even though he has been gone for many years, I have a sacred responsibility to hallow his name—to live up to the things he taught me, to try to be as good a man as he was, to live in such a way so that people who never knew him will look at me and say, "His father must have been a good man," and the people who knew my dad will say, "He's a credit to his father's name."

A GREATER NAME

But that is not the only name I bear. I have another patronymic attached to my name. As a Christian, I bear the name of my Heavenly Father. Hallowing his name means living in such a way that I increase his reputation in the world. When I've done it well, people who don't know God will look at my life and say, "He must have a great God," and God will look down from heaven with a smile and say, "That's my boy!"

Here is the simple application. It is in the form of a question: What can the world conclude about God by watching your life? Spend some time thinking about the answer.

When you pray, "Hallowed be your name," you are both the voice and the feet of that petition. As the very words leave your lips, your life is part of the answer. When you pray that God's name be hallowed, your first obligation is to live in such a way that God has no trouble answering your prayer.

GOING DEEPER

1. What is it about the Lord's Prayer that attracts the reverence and respect of even nonreligious people?

2. What is the first image that comes to mind when you hear the phrase "hallowed be your name"? Why is this petition difficult for most people to understand?

3. How does the *name* of God reflect who he is? What does it mean to take God's name lightly, or in vain? (See Exod. 20:7.)

PRAYER

Almighty God,

Root out everything in us that is false and untrue.

Set our feet to follow where you lead.

May our words and deeds, and even our secret thoughts, bring honor to your name.

Help us to live so that others find it easy to believe in you.

In Jesus' name.

Amen.

4. Take the Three Circles test. Draw three circles and put a throne in the center of each one. Where will you place the cross? Is Christ outside your life, inside your life but not on the throne, or on the throne of your life?

5. State in your own words what it means to *hallow* God's name. What items would you add to the list that begins, "God's name is not hallowed when . . ."?

6. Read Isaiah 6 out loud. How did Isaiah respond to a vision of God's holiness? How did this experience help him discover God's will for his life?

AN ACTION STEP

Spend an hour studying the names of God in the Old Testament. What do the following Scriptures teach us about the nature and character of God? Genesis 16:13; Genesis 17:1–2, Genesis 22:14; Exodus 15:22–26; Leviticus 20:8; Deuteronomy 32:18; Judges 6:24; Psalm 23:1; Psalm 46:7; Psalm 90:1–3; Jeremiah 23:5–6; Ezekiel 48:35.

A TRUTH TO REMEMBER:

God's name matters to God. It ought to matter to us.

"Your kingdom come."
MATTHEW 6:10

CHAPTER FOUR
KINGDOMS IN CONFLICT

Before we begin: What is the kingdom of God? In what sense is it a present reality? In what sense is it yet to come? How would things be different if you had a "God invasion" in your life? Your family? Your workplace? Your neighborhood?

SOMETIMES OUR PRAYERS ARE TOO small. Not long ago I was at a prayer meeting with the men who make up my Promise Keepers group. As we went around the circle, we shared our various needs. One man was going on a business trip soon, another had a son with problems in his English class, another mentioned a health issue in his family, and another asked us to pray about a troublesome situation at work. All the requests were legitimate. All were shared with a sense of honesty and openness.

As we began to pray, everything proceeded normally until one man prayed something like this: "Lord, teach us to pray big prayers. So much of what we pray is just details." I found that a helpful and challenging thought. It's not that the details don't matter. They do, but sometimes our prayers suffer because our vision is so small. If we truly want to honor God, we will believe what he says and then act on that belief by praying large prayers that require an Almighty God to answer them.

When we come to the second petition of the Lord's Prayer, it is as if God himself says, "Ask me for something hard. Ask me to send my kingdom to the earth." Now that's big. It's a lot bigger than asking God to give you a good time on your vacation to Florida or asking God for the right Christmas present for your cousin Sherrie. As we will see later in our journey through the Lord's Prayer, it's perfectly appropriate to bring even the tiniest concerns of life to our Heavenly Father. But if all we do is pray about small things, we have missed the world-changing power of the Lord's Prayer.

"Your kingdom come." That's serious business. On one level you are asking God to send Jesus back and bring down the curtain on human history as we have known it. On another level you are inviting God to invade your world and transform it. If that's of interest to you, then let's spend a few minutes thinking about what it means to pray this way.

I begin with two simple observations.

First, *this is the shortest petition in the Lord's Prayer.* In English, it is three words; in Greek, only four words. Don't be misled by that fact. Length does not indicate importance. In this case it indicates the opposite.

Second, *this is an imperative.* That means it is given in the form of a command. More than that, the verb is placed first for emphasis. You could rightfully translate it, "Come, kingdom of God." The same is true of the following petition, "Be done, will of God." When we pray, "Your kingdom come," there is an atmosphere of calm, steady faith about those words, as if we mean to say, "I know your kingdom is coming someday, and I pray that you will help me be patient until that day finally comes." And that sort of prayer is entirely biblical. We are called to wait patiently for the coming of the Lord. But when we pray, "Come, kingdom of God," there is a note of urgency about those words, as if we are praying, "Lord, let your kingdom come right here, right now, today!" To pray this way means that we are not satisfied with the status quo. We are praying because we know things could be, and should be, better than they are.

GOD'S GREAT SOCIETY

But what is this kingdom of God for which we are to pray? It's clearly a crucial topic, or Jesus wouldn't have mentioned it. A quick perusal of the Gospels—especially the synoptic Gospels (Matthew, Mark, and Luke) reveals that the phrases "kingdom of God" and "kingdom of heaven" are repeated over and over. A quick check through a concordance reveals that the word *kingdom* comes up over and over. Not just a few times but dozens and dozens of time. It is clear that Jesus talked to his disciples about the "kingdom of God" almost every day. It's no small subject. And Jesus said that when we pray, we are to petition God that the kingdom might "come."

What is the kingdom of God? Ask ten different theologians and you will receive ten different answers. For one thing the term is never precisely defined. In our thinking a kingdom requires a king and a realm in which he will rule. For a kingdom to be operative, the king must have people who are subject to his rule. And in the earthly sense a kingdom is more than a vague, undefined realm; it's also a literal piece of real estate. It always includes land, dirt, some sort of property with measurable boundaries. William Barclay offers this helpful definition: The kingdom of God is "a society upon earth in which God's will is as perfectly done as it is in heaven."[1] The kingdom of God is, first, a society, an organized group of men and women. It is, second, "on earth." It is, third, a place where the will of God is done.

But why is the kingdom of God so important? Why would Jesus speak of it over and over? Most importantly, why is the kingdom of God so important that we should make it the subject of our daily prayers?

That's a good question, and in this chapter I would like to offer four different answers.

THE KINGDOM IS CENTRAL

The first answer is this: *The kingdom of God is important because it was the central issue of Jesus' ministry.*

The kingdom of God is what he came to establish. He said that in various ways over and over. Consider the following verses:

> "From that time Jesus began to preach and say, 'Repent, the kingdom of heaven is at hand'" (Matt. 4:17 NASB)
>
> "Jesus was going over Galilee, . . . preaching the good news of the kingdom" (Matt. 4:23 HCSB).
>
> "I must proclaim the good news about the kingdom of God, . . . because I was sent for this purpose" (Luke 4:43 HCSB).
>
> "The kingdom of God is in your midst" (Luke 17:21 NASB).
>
> "My kingdom is not of this world. . . . My kingdom does not have its origin here." "You say that I'm a king," Jesus replied. "I was born for this, and I have come into the world for this: to testify to the truth. Everyone who is of the truth listens to My voice" (John 18:36–37 HCSB).

When Jesus began his ministry, he announced that the kingdom of God was "at hand" and "in your midst." He said that preaching the kingdom of God was the reason he had been sent to the earth. At the end of his ministry, he told Pontius Pilate that his kingdom was "not of this world" but was "from another place."

Jesus came to establish a new society on the earth. This society would be made up of men and women who are fully dedicated to doing the will of God. When he was here, the kingdom of God was "at hand" because the King himself was "in the midst" of the people. But the kingdom he would establish would be fundamentally different from the kingdoms of this world because it would call for a moral commitment from those who follow him. That's a crucial point that forever separates the kingdom of God from every earthly kingdom.

Being in an earthly kingdom is merely a matter of geography. It is, so to speak, just an accident of birth. Not so with Jesus' kingdom. As he said to Pilate, "Everyone who is of the truth listens to My voice" (John 18:37 HCSB). The kingdom of God is reserved for those who recognize and follow the truth as it is revealed in Jesus Christ. That's the moral commitment that Jesus demands of his followers. "You want to be in my kingdom? Fine. But you have to become a follower of the truth. You can't remain neutral about me or about the things I am saying. You have to get off the fence and make a commitment, or you'll never be in the kingdom of God."

And that explains why the people of the world will never understand the people of the kingdom. We have made a moral commitment to the truth, and that commitment guides everything we do. We start from a different place, we look at life in a different way, we make our decisions on a different basis, and therefore we end up in a different place. That fact applies all the way across the board, whether we are talking about how to raise our children, or how to spend our money, or how to vote in an election. Our commitment to truth forever separates us from the people of the world, which is why they don't understand us and think we're a little bit crazy. We aren't crazy, but we are different.

The kingdom of God is reserved for people who are fundamentally different from the people of the world.

Let's take that one step farther. The kingdom comes first in the hearts of men and women as they surrender themselves to Jesus Christ. That's where it all begins. But since that is true, we also know that kingdom spreads not through political power but through gentle persuasion as one by one people choose to follow Jesus Christ. As good and right and important as political action is, it can never by itself bring in the kingdom of God.

We ought to register to vote, we ought to write letters to our congressmen, we ought to speak out on moral issues, and we ought to run for office. But as good as those things are, they will never bring in the kingdom of God. The kingdom of God must come in human hearts before it will ever affect society at large. Conversion comes before character and personal change before social change. In the great debate concerning evangelism and social action, the answer must be that while both are needed, evangelism takes priority because it is only through the spreading of the gospel that human hearts are changed.

There is much more that might be said on this point, but to say this much at least makes clear why the kingdom of God was central to Jesus. It is the reason he came to earth. What was important to him must become important to us. And that's one reason Jesus taught us to pray, "Your kingdom come."

THE ETERNAL KINGDOM

There is a second reason Jesus taught us to pray this way: *The kingdom of God is the only thing that will last forever.*

When was the last time you thought about Zachary Taylor? It's probably been a long time. Until a few years ago the last time I thought about Zachary Taylor was back in Mrs. Alexander's eighth grade American history class, and I didn't think too much about him then. We were on vacation in Arizona and Utah when I happened to hear on the radio that they were digging up Zachary Taylor.

It had been so long since I thought about him that I had to stop and remember who he was. When the announcer called him "President Taylor," it sounded odd to me. I had never heard that expression before. It didn't sound right. The scientists dug up his remains to see if he had been poisoned with arsenic by his enemies. (It turns out the answer was no. He apparently died after eating some chilled cherries and cold buttermilk—a deadly combination.) Do you know what they found when they opened the casket? It had been 140 years since he died, and there wasn't much left. They found his hair, his bones, and his fingernails. Everything else had disintegrated.

"OLD ROUGH AND READY"

One newspaper said, "We now know more about Zachary Taylor than we ever knew before—and more than we ever wanted to know." Another story called him the most obscure president in American history because he was succeeded by a man whose name has become a sort of running Trivial Pursuit joke—Millard Fillmore.

Here's the oddity of it all. When he died, Zachary Taylor was considered a great man. One writer put things in perspective by calling him "the Norman Schwarzkopf of his day." He was a great military leader who later became president. He was the hero of the Battle of Buena Vista during the Mexican War. His nickname was "Old Rough and Ready," an appellation not much different from calling George Patton "Old Blood and Guts." Until they dug him up, we had forgotten Zachary Taylor altogether. One of our old hymns puts it this way:

> Time like an ever-rolling stream
> Bears all its sons away,
> They fly forgotten as the night
> Dies at the opening day.

Solomon added these words of wisdom in Ecclesiastes 9:5: "For the living know that they will die, but the dead know nothing; they have no further reward, *and even the memory of them is forgotten*." What a sobering thought—"even the memory of them is forgotten." It's true. Zachary Taylor had been forgotten, and he was once the president of the United States. After 150 years "Old Rough and Ready" is nothing more than the answer to a trivia question: "What president died after eating chilled cherries and cold buttermilk?" It is true of all human endeavors: "They fly forgotten as the night dies at the opening day."

What a lesson this is for all of us. If you are counting on somebody remembering you after you are gone, forget it. Sooner or later, you'll be just another name on a tombstone. Let me tell you what will happen after you die. Your family will call up the funeral home and arrange a nice service. Someone will stand up and say some nice things about you, and then they will bury you in the ground.

Do you know what happens then? Your friends will go over to your house and have a party and eat your food. Then they will get in their cars, go back home, and get on with their lives.

Somebody may say, "That's depressing." No, it's not. That's reality. And if I happen to die before you do, you'll do the same thing for me. And before long I'll just be a dim memory, and then I'll be forgotten altogether.

If you are looking for significance and permanence in this world, you are wasting your time. By definition this world forgets the past, lives in the present, and dreams about the future. And all those things we do to give ourselves significance—the degrees after our names, the houses we buy, the money we save, the cars we drive, the empires we build, the relationships we seek, the clothes we wear, the networks we create—in the end those things will amount to nothing. If you are living for this world, you are of all people most to be pitied.

Why? Because nothing in this world lasts forever. Just ask Zachary Taylor.

THE UNSHAKABLE KINGDOM

That's why Hebrews 12:28 says that God is going to give "a kingdom that cannot be shaken." Everything that is of this world is shakable. The buildings crumble into dust, companies go into bankruptcy, our degrees fade into illegibility, our houses age and creak and crumble, our cars rust out, and worst of all, our bodies eventually wear out. But the kingdom of God lasts forever.

When the angel Gabriel came to Mary, he predicted that she would give birth to a Son who would "reign over the house of

Jacob forever, *and His kingdom will have no end*" (Luke 1:33 HCSB). God desires to establish a kingdom on earth that will last forever. That kingdom will be made up of men and women who have decided to live by God's eternal values. Therefore, the whole human race may be divided into two groups—those who live by earthly values and those who live by kingdom values. If you decide to live by earthly values, you will receive an earthly reward. If you decide to live by kingdom values, you will receive a kingdom reward. The difference is this: Living by earthly values produces earthly rewards that pay off quicker and disappear faster; living by kingdom values produces kingdom rewards. They don't usually come as quickly, but they last forever.

You can live for this world, or you can live for the kingdom of God. The choice is yours.

That's the second reason the kingdom of God is so important. It's the only thing that will last forever.

KINGDOM PURPOSE

The third reason is this: *The kingdom of God gives purpose, meaning, and a goal to history.*

Where is history going? Philosophers have pondered that question for thousands of years. Is history nothing more than a tale told by an idiot, scribbled on the walls of an insane asylum? Or is history, as Edward Gibbon suggested, "little more than the register of crimes, follies, and misfortunes of mankind."[2] Should we accept the Hindu view that history is an endless cycle of reincarnation? Or should we adopt a vague evolutionary view that we came up from the slime over the course of billions and billions of years? Where would that lead us? To some positive-thinking nirvana where every day in every way things are getting better and better? Or should we conclude with the cynics that life is meaningless, an eternal cul-de-sac that leads to nothing at all?

No question is more important, because the way you view history ultimately shapes the way you view your own life. If you believe that history is going nowhere, then your life is just a momentary blip on the radar screen of the universe—you pop up, you fly across the screen, you disappear, never to be heard from again. If history has no goal, then life has no meaning, and every man is left to his own devices. When pornographer Larry Flynt was interviewed by Larry King, he said he believed we are like bottles on a conveyor belt. We pop up, ride the belt for a while, then something knocks us off the belt, and we disappear, and our place is taken by someone else. It would be hard to imagine a more hopeless view of human life.

HISTORY IS "HIS STORY"

The Bible teaches that history is *his* story, the record of God's dealings with the human race. It teaches that the universe had a definite beginning at a definite point in time. And it teaches that man didn't come up from the slime in some crazy accident of evolution. God created man with a purpose, and history is the story of the slow unfolding of God's purpose on the earth. The Old Testament prophets spoke again and again of a coming kingdom on the earth. Abraham caught a glimpse of it; Moses saw it from afar; David learned about it directly from God; and the major and minor prophets filled in the details. The Old

Testament writers foresaw a time when God's Messiah would rule the world from David's throne in Jerusalem.

If you put the pieces together, they speak of a coming golden age for the earth, a utopia if you will, a paradise on the earth itself. In that day the lion will lie down with the lamb, and all nations will stream into Jerusalem. The law of God will be written in the human heart, and "the earth will be full of the knowledge of the LORD as the waters cover the sea" (Isa. 11:9).

The New Testament writers add two significant details: (1) the promised Messiah is none other than the Lord Jesus Christ; (2) the kingdom of God will not be ultimately established until Jesus the King returns to the earth in person. And *that* is where history is going. The kingdom of God is what history is all about. It's the goal toward which everything else is moving. It's the last chapter in a story that started in the Garden of Eden.

Praying "your kingdom come" is a way of joining with the faithful of all ages who have surveyed the wreckage of a fallen world and concluded that there must be something better than this. We are looking through the haze of history to a time when the Lord Jesus Christ will reign on the earth in person. In a deep sense we are asking God to hasten the day when the Lord himself will descend from heaven and reclaim his rightful place as the ruler of the earth. That's why the angels declared to the startled apostles that "this same Jesus" who had ascended to heaven would one day return to the earth (Acts 1:11).

In many ways this is a shocking thought, one that runs against the grain of modern thinking. We believe that a man who once walked on the earth two thousand years ago, and who disappeared from the earth, is one day coming back to the earth. Who is he? "This same Jesus." The same one who walked the dusty roads of Judea and Galilee. The same one who healed the woman who touched the hem of his garment. The same one who divided the loaves and the fish and fed five thousand people. The same one who told a man named Nicodemus that he must be born again. The same one who caused the lame to walk and the blind to see. The same one who walked on the water. This same Jesus is one day returning to the earth. I could go on, but you get the idea.

Most of us have spent many years reading the Bible and looking at pictures of Jesus performing miracles and speaking to great multitudes. I can recall standing in the Hermitage museum in St. Petersburg, Russia, just a foot or so from Rembrandt's powerful painting of Christ being taken from the cross. We believe that the Jesus who is the subject of that painting, the one who died on the cross and rose from the dead, is actually, literally, bodily, physically, and personally returning to the earth one day. And he's not sending a representative. He's coming back in person. That's a mind-blowing fact. No wonder the skeptics think that Christians believe in fantasies. If you stop and ponder what we believe, it is truly an out-of-this-world truth.

TEN THOUSAND POINTS OF LIGHT

Let me give you a *Reader's Digest* version of what history is all about. In the beginning God created the heavens and the earth. He then placed Adam and Eve on the earth and made them stewards over the whole planet. But when they disobeyed, they surrendered their stewardship into the hands of Satan, God's archenemy. From that day until this, the whole world has been the domain of Satan. It is still God's world by creation. But Satan has usurped God's authority and set up a counterkingdom to the kingdom of God. And from that day until this, the earth has been the central battlefield in a war between those two competing kingdoms.

But that's not the whole story. Once the world fell into enemy hands, God determined to win it back at any cost. That meant sending his message through kings and prophets and priests and poets. It meant raising up an entire nation through whom he would bless the earth. But ultimately it meant that he himself had to enter the conflict. In order to reclaim the world from Satan, God entered the human race in the person of his Son, the Lord Jesus Christ.

That story is familiar to you, but perhaps you are not used to thinking of it as God's ultimate blow against Satan. Even then it appeared that Satan might win; indeed for thirty-six hours it seemed certain that he had won, that the battle was over, and God had been decisively defeated. Then Sunday came and, with it, the empty tomb and the risen Savior. Suddenly it became clear to everyone—even to Satan—that Jesus was the victor in the great battle to reclaim the earth. Since that first Easter Sunday, Satan has been like a squatter on planet earth. Jesus reclaimed the title deed, but Satan refused to give up his territory.

But, please mark very carefully four sub-facts on Satan's side. First, he refuses to acknowledge his defeat. Second,

> he refuses to surrender his dominion until he must. . . . Third, he is supported in his ambitions by man. He has man's consent to his control. The majority of men on the earth today, and in every day, have assented to his control. . . . Fourth, he hopes yet to make his possession of the earth permanent.[3]

The world is still in darkness, but here and there the followers of Jesus have established outposts of the kingdom, little pinpoints of light that promise better things to come. Meanwhile the battle rages on between the two kingdoms—King Jesus on one side and Satan on the other. In these last twenty centuries the light has spread until it seems like there are ten thousand points of light chasing away the darkness. In many other places, however, things look darker than ever.

That's the history of the world up until this present moment. But it is not the end of the story. All over the world, in those little outposts of the kingdom, the followers of Jesus are praying, "Your kingdom come," and as they do, they set their gaze toward the eastern sky and wait for the Son of God personally and visibly to return to the earth. When at last he comes, he will trample Satan under his feet, judge the workers of iniquity, set right the wrongs in the world, and reign from David's throne in Jerusalem. That day has not yet come, but it will come. Indeed it is coming, and we believe the "signs of the times" tell us that the coming of Christ is not far away. But whether near or far, the kingdom Jesus will establish on the earth forms the goal of all human history. It is the last and greatest chapter in the battle of the ages.

That's why the kingdom of God is all important, and that is why "your kingdom come" is the central petition of the Lord's Prayer. You are praying that God's whole program for human history might succeed and that Satan's counterkingdom might be destroyed.

KINGDOM LIVING

This is the fourth and final reason the kingdom of God is so important: *The kingdom of God is the only possible way to explain why some people live the way they do.*

It's also the reason that strikes the closest to home. Without the kingdom of God, it is simply impossible to explain the way some people choose to live. There are men and women all around us who, although they seem perfectly normal as the world counts normality, in some ways seem to behave differently.

I submit to you that when you examine their lives, the one great factor that makes a difference is that they have been gripped with the concept of the kingdom of God. They have decided to "seek first the kingdom of God," and that has made all the difference in the world.

Should that surprise us? No, because Jesus predicted that some people would choose to live that way. These are his words in Luke 18:29–30: "I assure you: There is no one who has left a house, wife or brothers, parents or children because of the kingdom of God, who will not receive many times more at this time, and eternal life in the age to come" (HCSB). Jesus is teaching us that the kingdom of God changes the values of life. It leads to unusual and otherwise unexplainable behavior.

When you sign up for Christ's kingdom, you parachute directly into a war zone.[4] You are leaving a life that makes sense (from the world's point of view) for a life governed by eternal realities. People will do things because of the kingdom of God that they would not do otherwise. In some cases they will choose to set aside a life of ease and comfort; in other cases they will set aside the closest human relationships; in still other cases they will give up a promising career; still others will spend their money in ways that make no earthly sense.

I have some friends who have just started their second term as medical missionaries in Nigeria. Both are doctors who had well-established practices in America. A few years ago they felt God calling them to put their careers on hold and to serve in a hospital in Jos, Nigeria. They have four children who went with them. My wife and I (along with my bother Alan) visited them during their first term.

It is hard for those of us who are used to advanced medical care to comprehend the working conditions in Africa. The day we arrived the hospital ran out of sutures. Does that ever happen in America? I can't imagine a major medical facility in the States where they would suddenly say, "We can't do surgery because we don't have any sutures to sew up the patient." But Greg and Carolyn Kirschner weren't surprised. That sort of thing happens all the time in Africa.

They had two X-ray machines, but one of them was not working. Everything was primitive by American standards. The

Kirschners also weren't surprised to learn that my brother Alan had brought with him a large supply of sutures donated by a hospital in Tupelo, Mississippi. To them, it was no coincidence that a visitor brought what they needed on the very day they ran out of supplies. That's what life is like on the mission field. It's not just George Müller of Bristol who lived day by day, praying for whatever those orphans needed. That's how they operate at the Evangel Hospital in Jos, Nigeria. And that's how it is on mission stations all over the world.

But couldn't Greg and Carolyn make more money by staying in America? Yes, and they could spend that money in support of other missionaries. And their children would be closer to their grandparents, too. They were back in the States for almost two years. Going back the second time in some ways is harder. All the romance has been washed away by the hard reality of life in Nigeria.

It's not that it's a bad place to live or that they don't like it there. Not at all. They love the opportunity of using their considerable gifts to serve others in the name of Jesus Christ. But it is different, and as Greg pointed out to me, in Nigeria you are always reminded that you are a resident alien.

So why go back a second time? Because Greg and Carolyn Kirschner have decided to live by kingdom values. They are "leaving home" for the sake of the kingdom of God in the belief that the words of Jesus are literally true. They have been captured by a higher calling. That's why they went in the first place. And that's why they are going back.

Let me take this a step further. Jesus laid down the challenge in even starker terms in Luke 14:26: "If anyone comes to Me and does not hate his own father and mother, wife and children, brothers and sisters—yes, and even his own life—he cannot be My disciple" (HCSB). You can check the word *hate* in the Greek, and you'll discover that hate is exactly what it means. But the *hate* of this verse doesn't refer to personal animosity. Being faithful to Jesus Christ and following his call on your life may mean that from time to time you will do things that seem to your loved ones as if you hate them. You don't hate them at all, but your obedience to Christ may cause them to think that you hate them. Such is the price we all must pay to be a disciple of Christ.

YOU'LL NEVER KNOW UNTIL YOU PRAY THE PRAYER

Am I suggesting that living for kingdom values means going to the mission field? Not really. But that does stand as a particularly good example. It throws into bold relief what seeking first the kingdom of God is all about. If you ever decide to make the kingdom of God the first priority in your life, you may not become a missionary, but you will become fundamentally different from the world around you. And the choices you make in your own life will be continually misunderstood because you will be living for values that the people of the world don't comprehend. Perhaps that seems too intimidating. I hope not.

Even though you decide to make the kingdom of God your first priority, your life may seem mundane. That's all right. You don't need to go to Nepal or Swaziland or Bulgaria to live for the kingdom of God. You don't even have to move to another country. The kingdom of God is not a matter of geography; it's a matter of the heart. You become a kingdom man or a kingdom woman when you decide to live by the values that matter to God—righteousness, holiness, humility, compassion, zeal, sacrifice, charity, joy, and forgiveness.

Consider the matter this way. Every time you pray, you must say one of two things. Either you pray, "Your kingdom come," or you pray, "My kingdom come." Those are the only two possibilities. But note carefully: When you pray "Your kingdom come," you must of necessity also pray, "My kingdom go." God's kingdom cannot "come" unless your kingdom is going to "go." They both can't coexist at the same time and place. The bottom line is this: Those who pray, "Your kingdom come" will never be sorry. We have the words of Jesus on that. Whatever they lose will be amply repaid in this life and in the life to come. But you'll never know until you pray that prayer.

FOUR WAYS TO PRAY

Let me wrap this up by suggesting four ways to pray, "Your kingdom come."[5]

1. *In your own life.* It all begins here. Jesus said, "I assure you: Whoever does not welcome the kingdom of God like a little child will never enter it" (Luke 18:17 HCSB). You enter the kingdom of God by having the simple faith of a child. You enter the kingdom by asking the Lord Jesus to become King in your life. So we must ask a crucial question: *Are you in the kingdom of God?* The answer must always be yes or no.

You enter the kingdom through simple faith in King Jesus. But—and note this carefully!—you enter individually and personally. No one else can enter for you. It requires a definite decision on your part. Without that definite decision, you will not even "see" the kingdom of God (John 3:3).

So we begin there. Are you in the kingdom of God? If the answer is yes, then you pray a prayer like this every day: "Lord Jesus, may your kingdom come in my life today. May your values dominate my thinking and my decision making. May your cause in the world be advanced by the things I say and do. Help me to do your will all through this day."

There's no magic in that prayer, but properly understood it is a revolutionary way to pray. Make no mistake. If you mean those words, God will take you up on your offer to become a "kingdom person." Don't pray like this if you intend to stay the way you are.

2. *In your family.* That means praying for your wife, your husband, and your children that they too would become kingdom people. This includes praying for your extended family and even for the spouses that your children and grandchildren will one day marry.

3. *In your church.* The church is to be a model of that "great society" God is building. Even the best church will fall far short of the ideal. But why not pray for your pastor, the staff, elders and deacons, and the various committees that they will be completely committed to kingdom values? And then pray for the congregation, that men and women would set aside their own agenda. The church can become as political as any political

party. Differences of opinion are good and healthy, but sometimes we can get so fixated on our own ideas that we destroy the unity of the Spirit in our desire to get our own plans implemented. Pray that your church will become an attractive community of kingdom people—an outpost of light in an ever-darkening world.

4. *In the world.* It's true that the kingdom will not ultimately come until the King himself returns to the earth. Yet the kingdom of God comes in a spiritual sense as men and women surrender their lives to King Jesus. So we are praying, "May your kingdom come in hearts and lives today, and may the King himself quickly return." While you are at it, pray for the kingdom to come in your community, your state, your nation, and finally throughout the world. "O God, give us leaders who fear your name and respect your law." As you pray, remember the words of Proverbs 14:34, "Righteousness exalts a nation, but sin is a disgrace to any people."

"BEGIN, I PRAY THEE, WITH ME"

I conclude with this final observation: "Your kingdom come" is not a passive prayer. It's not a placebo for someone who wants to stand by and watch the action from the grandstands. No, this is a prayer for someone who wants to get in the game. That's why the verb is an imperative—"Come, kingdom of God!"

Do you really want the kingdom of God to come? If you do, I leave you to ponder the words of this ancient Chinese prayer: "O Lord, change the world. Begin, I pray thee, with me."

PRAYER

Father,

We thank you that Satan will not have the last word.

Come, Lord Jesus, come quickly and establish your visible kingdom on the earth.

Between now and then help us to live as kingdom people whose values are not of this world.

May we not grow accustomed to second-best living when you have called us to higher ground.

Grant us wisdom to be citizens of heaven while we sojourn as pilgrims on the earth.

In Jesus' name.

Amen.

GOING DEEPER

A TRUTH TO REMEMBER:
If you ever decide to make the kingdom of God your first priority, you will become fundamentally different from the world around you.

1. When we pray, "Come, kingdom of God!" what are we really praying for? How will we know when our prayer has been answered?

2. Why did Jesus talk so much about the kingdom of God?

3. What does this petition suggest about the attempt to improve the world through legislation and political pressure? How can we strive for what is right while at the same time praying, "Your kingdom come"? How does this petition impart a sense of humility to our efforts to make the world a better place?

4. Describe the difference between a life lived by worldly values and a life lived by kingdom values.

5. How does Satan try to stop God's kingdom from spreading in the world today? How does he attack you personally?

6. Memorize Luke 18:29–30. Ask God to help you live for the sake of his kingdom this week.

AN ACTION STEP

This chapter ends with four ways to pray "Your kingdom come." Use that as a guide in your personal prayer time for the next seven days.

"Your will be done on earth as it is in heaven."
MATTHEW 6:10

CHAPTER FIVE

NOTHING MORE, NOTHING LESS, NOTHING ELSE

Before we begin: Why is it difficult to sincerely pray, "Your will be done"? How would your life change if doing God's will became your first priority?

SOME PRAYERS ARE HARDER TO PRAY than others. I learned that many years ago when my father died. One October day he felt a pain in his shoulder. The doctors later said it was transferred pain from a bacterial infection in his liver. It did not seem serious at first, but he got no better, and a few days later traveled by ambulance to Birmingham, where a battery of doctors went to work on him. Marlene and I drove in from Dallas, arriving at the hospital sometime after midnight.

Dad spoke to me when I saw him, but I could tell he was desperately ill.

A few days later, now back in Dallas, the dreaded call came. Once again we sped through the night to Birmingham, hoping against hope. But I could tell he was not long for this world. That day—it is etched forever in my mind—I went in to see him, and he did not know me. He was drugged and nearly in a coma. Outside the intensive care unit I saw a friend from my childhood days. Somehow seeing an old friend triggered emotions I had kept bottled up inside.

Leaning against the wall, I wept furious tears, unable to keep back the truth—my father was dying, and I could do nothing about it. I must have prayed that day. I'm sure I did. After all, I was in seminary learning to help other people draw near to God. But if I prayed, I do not remember it. In that terrible moment of utter helplessness, prayer did not come naturally. All theology aside, I knew my father was dying. I could hardly pray, "O God, heal him," for I knew in my soul that that prayer on that day was not going to be answered. But I could not pray, "O God, take him home and end the pain," for he was my father and much too young to die. So I prayed something, exactly what I do not remember. In a few days God mercifully intervened and ended my father's ordeal.

PRAYING IN THE DARKNESS

When I first started in the ministry, I hesitated to share that story because it seemed too personal. Over the years I came to understand that nearly everyone is in a similar situation sooner or later. You have stood beside the bed of a loved one and found that prayer was nearly impossible. Or you have faced a difficulty so immense that you truly did not know what words to use when you prayed. Or perhaps there have been times in your life when you have not prayed because you were afraid of the answer God would give.

Prayer can do that to even the best of us. It seems so easy on Sunday morning. Why is it so hard when the hard times come? Perhaps we are afraid of what God will say in response to our prayers. What if we ask for guidance, and he guides us in a way we don't want to go? What if we pray for wisdom and the wisdom we receive seems more like nonsense? What if we pray for patience and the answer means nothing but trouble for us?

This should not surprise us. Jesus hinted at the problem when he gave us the Lord's Prayer. Included in that model prayer were these words: "Your will be done on earth as it is in heaven." The basic difficulty may be easily seen if we lay it out in a series of logical statements:

- God has a will concerning my life.
- God's will encompasses his desires for my life.
- But I also have a will that encompasses my desires for my life.
- Those two wills will often (not always) be in conflict.
- When there is conflict, either God's will or my will must prevail.
- When I pray "Your will be done," I am asking that God's will prevail over my will.

That's the basic difficulty we face when we come to this petition. When we ask that God's will be done, we are implicitly asking that our wills be overturned, if necessary. That's good theory, but it's not easy to pray that way standing by the bedside of someone you love.

But that's only part of the problem. Jesus taught us to pray that God's will be done "on earth as it is in heaven." Exactly how is God's will being done in heaven? If the reference is to the angels, as I think it is, then God's will is *always* being done in heaven. Psalm 103:20 says, "Praise the LORD, you his angels, you mighty ones *who do his bidding, who obey his word.*" In heaven, God's will is *always* done; in heaven, God's will is *instantaneously* done; in heaven, God's will is *completely* done; in heaven, God's will is *joyfully* done. In essence, Jesus asks us to pray that we might become a little more like the angels, who always obey, and a little less like the demons, who never obey. When that happens, the earth will become a little more like heaven and a little less like hell.

HE WON'T CROSS THE PICKET LINE

But it rarely happens. God's will is rarely done on the earth. After all, there are more than six billion wills on the earth and still only one will in heaven. Just look around you. Do you see God's will being done? Pick up the newspaper and read about a school shooting in Colorado. Read about the rising bloodshed between the Jews and the Palestinians. In recent years our papers have been full of sordid tales of sexual misdeeds by the top elected officials in our land. As I write these words, there is news about a ballplayer being sentenced for drug abuse. On and on the stories go. A fair reading of the situation suggests that someone else's will is being done.

In some ways, "Thy will be done" seems like the most hopeless of all prayer requests. Rarely do we mean it. All too rarely does it seem to be answered. But the hardest part is this: God never burglarizes the human will. He is a perfect gentleman. He will not force himself upon you. If you do not wish to do his will, he will respect your decision. In the words of James Jauncey, "He will never cross the picket line of our unwillingness."

"Thy will be done" is a difficult prayer to pray sincerely. Those four one-syllable words may be the hardest prayer you will ever pray. Let's think together about what it means to ask that God's will be done on earth as it is in heaven.

TURNING OVER CONTROL

Praying "your will be done" means giving up control of your own life. We're back to that little syllogism again:

- God has a will (or desire) for your life.
- But you also have a will (or desire) for your life.
- When you pray, "Your will be done," you are asking that his will take precedence over your will.

Only one will can be done at a time. Either God calls the shots, or you call the shots. Either he is in control, or you are in control. It's not easy to pray like that because it means you have to give up control of your own life.

But you aren't really in control anyway; it only seems that way.

PROVERBS 20:4

A few years ago a Greek professor at Moody Bible Institute performed a wedding ceremony at the church I pastor. During a brief chat he brought up a verse I had never considered before—Proverbs 20:24, "A man's steps are directed by the LORD. How then can anyone understand his own way?" That didn't seem like a remarkable verse, until the professor mentioned one little fact. The word for *man* in the first part of the verse is a Hebrew word that means "a mighty warrior." The Old Testament writers used it to speak of soldiers who valiantly march into battle. These were the "mighty men" of Israel of great strength and courage. And Solomon says even their steps are directed by God. In fact, we could legitimately translate the first part of the verse this way: "Even the steps of a mighty man are directed by the Lord."

Think of the "mighty men" of today. Their names are Powell, Bush, Blair, Putin, and in another category Jordan, Woods, Sosa, and in yet another category Greenspan, Gates, Case, and Buffett. They appear to be self-made men, self-sufficient, able to run their own lives. But it only appears that way. Solomon says that behind the power and image of the mighty man stands the Lord himself. He is the one who directs their paths. And those "mighty men" are mighty only as God wills it. Here's proof. That list will be outdated almost by the time this book appears in print. And in ten years some people will read those names and say, "Who is he talking about?" The "mighty men" come and go. Only God remains forever.

That brings us to the second half of that verse: "How then can anyone understand his own way?" The word for *anyone* is the ordinary Hebrew word for *man.* If even the mighty man cannot direct his own steps, how then can any of us be sure about the future? If the people we look up to are at the mercy of Higher Hands, then how can any of us claim to understand fully the direction of our lives? The answer is, we can't. The mighty man can't. The average man can't. You can't. I can't. No one can.

Just when we think we've got the world by the tail on a downhill slide, everything falls to pieces.

WHAT JIM BAKKER LEARNED IN PRISON

Not many years ago Jim Bakker was one of the most important Christian leaders in America. As the founder of the PTL ministries, he presided over one of the largest broadcasting empires in the world. Millions of people watched him on television every day. Then came the fall. First, there was the revelation of the affair with Jessica Hahn. Then came accusations of greed, fraud, and further sexual misconduct. It all eventually led to a trial that ended in a prison sentence. Jim Bakker suffered a nervous breakdown that was trumpeted from coast to coast. After going to prison, he suffered the final blow when his wife divorced him and married one of his former best friends.

Few Christian leaders in recent history have fallen so far so fast. I remember watching his program in the 1980s, and I also followed the details of the collapse of his vast empire. When he went to prison, I simply forgot about him. But God didn't. That much is evident from a book he wrote called *I Was Wrong.* After being released from prison several years ago, Jim Bakker wrote about the events leading to his fall and the things that happened while he was in prison. After writing at some length about the total despair and humiliation he felt, he described a singular moment when he simply began to read the Bible. He cried out, "God, why am I here? There are so many dying men in prison. How can I help them?" The answer from the Lord surprised him. "You are arrogant. You think you are the only person I have in this prison. I have many others here. I am God. I did not bring you to prison to minister. I brought you here to know me."[1]

That was the turning point. By his own admission he had been an extremely ambitious man. After climbing to the pinnacle of evangelical success, he ended up losing everything. Little by little God stripped it all away and left him with nothing but guilt, pain, and failure. When he finally hit rock bottom, Jim Bakker met God in a new way. What he learned in prison, we must all learn sooner or later. The only thing that matters is knowing God and doing his will. When we truly pray, "Your will be done," things almost certainly won't work out the way we planned. And some things will end up opposite of what we expected. But that doesn't mean your life will go out of control. It just means that your life will now be consciously passed into God's control.

TRUSTING GOD

Praying "your will be done" means trusting God to do whatever he thinks is best. More than once I have heard people say, "Pray for the opposite of what you want, because God always gives us the opposite of what we ask." We laugh when we read that because it seems so absurd. But how many of us secretly wonder if it isn't true? We've all known the frustration of unanswered prayer. Perhaps it was for something small—like a new dress for a Saturday night date. Perhaps it was for God to give you a basset hound. Perhaps you asked God to open the door for you to go to a certain college. Or perhaps it was for something truly big—prayer requested at the bedside of a loved one, prayer for a sick child, prayer for a failing marriage. When God doesn't answer our prayers—or when he doesn't answer in the way we want—are we not tempted to wonder if maybe it's true that God always gives us the opposite of what we ask?

DOES GOD KNOW MY NAME?

Our biggest problem is not knowing whether there is a God because virtually everyone agrees that the answer is yes. Even people who never come to church and people who consider themselves irreligious would answer yes. The real questions are these: Is there a God in heaven who cares for me? *Does God know my name?* Does he understand my problems? Does he have any interest in me? Does he see my struggles? Does he feel my pain? Does he care what happens to me? Millions of people—including millions of apparently loyal churchgoers—secretly wonder if the answer to those questions must be no. A God who is there—yes. A God who cares for me—maybe not.

Perhaps some wonder if this does not reveal a kind of spiritual schizophrenia. How can you answer *yes* to one question and *no* or *maybe not* to the other? Is this not some kind of internal contradiction? If there is a God, surely he cares for me. And if he doesn't care for me, who cares whether there's a God or not? But the questions move on two different levels. The existence of God is primarily a mental or logical problem. It's an issue of philosophy. The question concerning God's personal concern is entirely different. Very often it is asked by those who have known deep pain and suffering. For them the question is very personal: If God cares for me, how could he let my son die? Or, where was God when my husband lost his job? Or, why didn't God stop that man who shot my father? These are not abstract questions about first causes and the argument from design. These are questions wrenched from the depths of horrible despair.

How do you pray "Your will be done" when you aren't sure that God really cares for you? If you knew—really knew—that he had your best interests at heart, you might dare to pray that way. But as long as you doubt, that prayer will be almost impossible.

HE BOWED HIS HEAD AND DIED

There are many answers to the question, Does God really care for me? But there is only one that really matters. It's the answer God gave two thousand years ago on a hill outside the city walls of Jerusalem. On a hot Friday afternoon the Romans crucified a man they thought to be a Jewish rabble-rouser. Only later did they understand who he really was.

His name was Jesus. He came from a small town in Galilee called Nazareth. He started his ministry by preaching in the synagogues. As he went from village to village, his fame spread until thousands came out to hear him. At length the powers-that-be found him to be a threat to them, and they decided to eliminate him. It took a long time to trap him, but they finally arrested him with the help of a traitor from his inner circle. Once arrested, he was tried, beaten, mocked, insulted, cursed, abused, slapped, scourged, and crowned with thorns. Eventually he was condemned to die. For six hours he hung on the cross—naked before the world, exposed before the elements, reviled by the crowd, jeered by his enemies, mourned by those who loved him. At the end, after suffering excruciating pain, he bowed his head and died.

And God said, "Do you still wonder if I love you?"

For some people even the death of God's Son will not be enough. But if that is not enough, then nothing God can do will make any difference. For if a man will give his own son to die, is there anything else he will hold back? Money is nothing compared to a son.

That's why the most crucial word of the Lord's Prayer is in the very first phrase, "Our *Father* in heaven." To call God "Father" means that you recognize what he did when he gave his own Son to die on the cross. He knows what it is to lose a son; he knows about pain and suffering; he knows the anguish of unjust accusations; he knows all about hatred; he knows about death. He's seen it up close and personal. He watched his Son die in agony. *Father* is not some word to flip around when we pray. It's what Christian prayer is all about. God is worthy to be called "Father" precisely because he has done what good fathers must do; he has sacrificed the best that he had for the welfare of his own children.

Look to the cross. Gaze on the Son of God. Ponder the meaning of Golgotha. Who is that crucified on Calvary's tree? His name is Jesus. Study his face. See the wounds in his hands, his feet, his side. Was it not for you that he died? Do you still doubt that God loves you?

People who have been abused sexually or physically or emotionally have a difficult time praying "your will be done." They fear what God will do to them. There is no easy answer to this problem. Since the problem is not intellectual, it won't be met by arguing at the intellectual level. Deep issues must be faced; bad memories must be confronted. These problems are best dealt with in a group setting. When believers pray together, good things happen that can lead to healing and emotional health.[2]

FACING SUFFERING AND PAIN

Praying "your will be done" means we may face suffering and pain. It was true for Jesus. The scene has shifted to Thursday night. It is late—perhaps 10:30 or 11 P.M. The Lord now retreats to his favorite spot—the olive groves in Gethsemane. Leaving Peter, James, and John behind, he wrestles in prayer with what is about to happen. He knows with the perfect knowledge of omniscience that the time has come for him to die. All is revealed; nothing is hidden. For this moment he came into the world. Nothing will surprise him—not Judas's wicked kiss, not Caiaphas's mocking words, not Pilate's curious questions. The pain, the blood, the anguish—all of it is seen as clearly to him as if it had already happened.

Most of all he sees the blackness. Sin like a dark cloud is lowering upon him. Sin! The word is repugnant to him. Sin in all its ugliness, all its vile reaches, all its putrefying force now looms before him. It is as if a giant sewer is being opened and the foul contents are flooding over him. All the evil that men can do, all the filth of uncounted atrocities, the swill of the human race, the total iniquity of every man and woman from the beginning of time.

As Jesus sees the cup filled with human scum approaching him, he recoils in horror. These are his words: "My Father! If it is possible, let this cup pass from Me. Yet not as I will, but as You will" (Matt. 26:39 HCSB).

These are not the words of unbelief. They are words of faith. They are the words of a man who understands fully what it will cost to do the will of God.

Was it wrong for Jesus to pray this way? Did it somehow reveal a lack of trust in God? I think not. No man was ever more committed to doing the will of God. He did not pray because he wished to be released from the will of God. He prayed because he knew how much the will of God would cost him personally. He was willing to pay the price, but in the horror of seeing the "cup" of suffering draw near, he asked that it might be removed from him. If Jesus struggled with the will of God, should we be surprised if we do the same? If it was difficult for Jesus to pray "Your will be done," is it likely to be any easier for us? Jesus is Exhibit A of what it costs to pray "Your will be done." It cost him his life. No wonder he struggled in Gethsemane.

A SOVEREIGN BULLET

I am writing these words just a few weeks after the tragic crash of a missionary airplane in Peru in which a mother and her seven-month-old daughter were shot to death with the same bullet fired from a Peruvian Air Force jet. Evidently the pilot of the jet mistook the missionaries for drug smugglers and shot the plane out of the sky. Out of more than fifty bullets that hit the missionary airplane, one particular bullet passed through the fuselage, hit Roni Bowers in the back, passed through her body, and lodged in the head of her daughter Charity, killing both mother and daughter instantly. Jim Bowers, Roni's husband, and Cory Bowers, Charity's brother, survived the crash.

For days afterward the major media gave massive coverage to the sad story. The world doesn't understand why missionaries do what they do. Why would fine people like Jim and Roni Bowers put themselves and their children in harm's way? Are there not safer places they could go? Why not stay in America?

The answer is simple and profound. They went because Jesus called them to go, and when Jesus calls, you go. Period. End of story. They went because they wanted to be part of God's harvest in a remote region of Peru. Did they know the risks? Absolutely. Was it an easy decision? No, it wasn't. But they knew the Lord was calling, and they were certain that the Lord was with them every step of the way. They went in obedience, trusting God to take care of them. Nothing that happened when their plane was shot out of the sky changes that truth in the least.

Thirteen hundred people attended the funeral service for Roni and Charity Bowers. There was a taped message from Elizabeth Elliot, whose husband Jim Elliot was killed by Auca tribesmen in Ecuador in 1956. Steve Saint, son of one of the other missionaries killed in 1956, spoke in person. Eventually Jim Bowers gave his first public comments since the plane crash.

After thanking a number of people, he made this remarkable statement:

> Most of all I want to thank my God. He's a sovereign God. We're finding that out more now. Some of you might ask, why thank God? Of course now, after hearing some people speak tonight, you're realizing why, maybe. Could this really be God's plan for Roni and Charity? God's plan for Cory and me and our family? And I'd like to tell you why I believe so, why I'm coming to believe so.

His list of reasons included many items, but I was struck by one in particular. His wife and daughter were killed by the same bullet. Stop and think about that for a moment. What are the chances—humanly speaking—that a bullet could be fired from a speeding jet, pass through the fuselage of the missionary airplane, hit Roni Bowers in the back, go through her heart, and then end up in the head of the baby she was holding in her lap? The best marksman in the world could never make that shot on purpose. It had to be more than chance. In his remarks Jim Bowers called it a "sovereign bullet." What an amazing thing to say. A sovereign bullet. Meaning that God was there, he was not absent, he knew everything that was happening, and he could have intervened in a thousand different ways to stop that bullet from hitting Roni and Charity. But he didn't. Only a man of biblical faith could have called it a "sovereign bullet."

Why did it happen? The full explanation is hidden in the heart and mind of God. But Jim Bowers said he believed God allowed the tragedy to wake up a sleeping church: "I think he also wanted to wake up sleeping Christians, including myself, and maybe most of all, to wake up those who have no interest or little interest in God. And I say tonight, wake up!"

"IT WILL BE WORTH IT ALL"

A few days before her death, Roni Bowers wrote her personal testimony, intending to send it to a few friends and family members. Little did she know it would soon be spread around the world. In it she speaks about her spiritual journey over the years and concludes with the story of how she was unable to have children of her own, despite repeated attempts. That's why she and Jim adopted Cory and Charity. She concludes with these moving words that in retrospect seem strangely prophetic: "Now I choose to trust God fully. He is in control; he knows what is best. He doesn't owe me anything, rather I owe him everything. When we as believers get to heaven, we won't have to ask, 'why?' It will be worth it all."[3]

So it has come to pass as the Lord ordained. Through her death Roni Bowers has touched people around the world, far more than she would have touched if she had survived the crash. And Jim Bowers is right. Through this tragedy God has spoken to multitudes of people—believers and unbelievers alike. Out of death has come life and a wake-up call to a sleeping generation. Was God's will done in this tragedy? If we believe in a "sovereign bullet," then the answer must be yes. In the coast guard, before a dangerous mission begins, the sailors are taught, "You have to go; you don't have to come back." The crash of the missionary airplane in the Amazon River proves once again the truth of those words. When Christ calls, we have to go. We don't have to come back.

AGAINST THE STATUS QUO

Praying "your will be done" means praying against the status quo.

God's will is seldom done on the earth. Too many things that go on are obviously not God's will.

- Killing the unborn is not God's will.
- Homosexuality is not God's will.
- The rising tide of divorce is not God's will.
- Single moms raising children is not God's will.
- Pastors committing adultery is not God's will.
- Rampant pornography is not God's will.
- Nuclear warfare is not God's will.
- Ethnic cleansing is not God's will.
- Racial prejudice is not God's will.
- Serial killings are not God's will.
- Greed, graft, and corruption are not God's will.

Sometimes it seems as if God has gone to sleep and Satan has taken over.

GOD DOES NOT ACCEPT THE STATUS QUO

Now ponder the next sentence carefully: *God does not accept the status quo.* He does not accept Satan's usurpation of God's rightful place in the world. He does not accept that sin should reign forever on the earth. He does not accept that the killing should go on forever. God does not sit idly by while the world goes to hell. That's why he sent the prophets, who thundered out his message to ancient Israel. That's why he raised up mighty men like Moses, Joshua, and David. That's why he inspired his prophets to write down his words. That's why he wrote the Ten Commandments with his own fingers.

God does not accept the status quo!

Do you want more proof? He sent his own Son into the world to change the status quo. What the prophets couldn't accomplish with their words, his Son accomplished by the Incarnation. At Bethlehem God sent a message to the world: "Things are going to change." If things were OK, why did God send his Son? But things weren't OK. They were wrong, dreadfully wrong, and getting worse all the time. So God intervened in human history in the most dramatic fashion possible.

To pray "Your will be done" is to follow God in opposing the status quo. This prayer goes against the grain. In a world where God's will is *not* done, you are to pray that God's will be done. Those are fighting words, words that rebel against everything that is evil and wrong on planet earth. All too often when we pray "Your will be done," we do it with an air of pious resignation. "O God, since I am helpless to stem the tide of events, may your will be done." Sometimes we use it as an excuse not to get angry at the sin and suffering all around us.

But if God does not accept the status quo, neither should we.

THE HAWK AND THE SWALLOWS

I confess that I hadn't thought much about this aspect of the prayer until I read a column by Alden Thompson. He points out that praying "your will be done" is to mount a massive offensive against all that is evil and crooked in the world. Too often we say these words with a kind of passive resignation, as if we really meant, "Your will be done, but we know things will never change anyway." We live in the "in between time" where Christ has come and gone and will one day come back again. The King announced his kingdom, then disappeared from the earth.

We know that better days are coming, but they aren't here yet. We live in a world with too much killing, too many broken marriages, too much greed, and too many broken promises. Thompson speaks of watching some swallows that built a nest on the back patio of his home. Day after day he and his family watched the swallows come and go. Five baby swallows hatched one spring day. Five weeks later a hawk swooped from the sky and took all five baby swallows away. Writing about it later, he spoke of the anger he felt: "At breakfast I stare at an empty nest. Then I go to my desk and write about Jesus' prayer, 'Thy will be done.' And I am angry, for the enemy doesn't restrict his visits to the nests of birds."[4]

Praying "your will be done" is an act of God-ordained rebellion. This is not a prayer for the weak or the timid. This is a prayer for troublemakers and rabble-rousers. It is a prayer for believers who look at the devastation all around them and who say, "I'm angry, and I'm not going to take this anymore." It is a prayer that leads necessarily to action. If you see injustice being done, you cannot blithely pray, "Your will be done," and then walk away. If you really mean "Your will be done," you've got to jump into the fray and help make it happen.

Let me summarize this point with two simple statements:

1. By means of humble prayer and fierce action, God's will *is* done on earth.

2. As God's will is done, the atmosphere of heaven is recreated on the earth.

YOU'LL NEVER KNOW TILL YOU LET GO

Let me summarize everything I've said in this chapter. Praying "your will be done" means at least four things:

1. Giving up control of your own life.
2. Trusting God to do whatever he thinks is best.
3. Accepting that personal pain and suffering may be part of God's will.
4. Refusing to accept the status quo.

I freely admit that this is not easy to do. And yet Jesus told us to pray this way. It's not wrong to struggle with this prayer. After all, Jesus struggled with it himself. But over the years I've discovered that the happiest people are those who have said, "I've decided to let go and let God run my life."

So many of us go through life with a clenched fist, trying to control the uncontrollable, trying to mastermind all the circumstances, trying to make our plans work. So we hold tightly to the things we value—our career, our reputation, our happiness, our health, our children, our education, our wealth, our possessions, and our mates. We even hold tightly to life itself. But those things we hold so tightly never really belonged to us. They always belonged to God. He loaned them to us, and when the time comes, he will take them back again.

Happy are those people who hold lightly the things they value greatly. The happiest people I know are the folks who have said, "All right, Lord. I'm letting go. I'm going to relax now and let you take over." What are you struggling with today? What are you holding on to so tightly that it almost makes your hands hurt? What is it that you are afraid to give up to God? Whatever it is, you'll be a lot happier when you finally say, "Your will be done," and then open your clenched fist. But you'll never know till you let go.

A SIMPLE PRAYER

Here's a simple prayer that may help you loosen your grip on the things with which you are struggling:

> Lord Jesus, may your will be done in my life.
>
> Nothing more,
> Nothing less,
> Nothing else. Amen.

Are you ready to let go of whatever stands between you and God? Count the cost. Take a deep breath. Only the brave will pray, "Your will be done." Those four words have the power to change your life and your world forever.

A TRUTH TO REMEMBER:

To pray, "Your will be done," is an act of God-ordained rebellion against the evil of this world.

PRAYER

Lord Jesus,

You have made it so simple that we can't miss the truth even if we tried.

You taught us to pray like this, and you showed us how when you prayed alone in the garden.

Forgive us for doubting your goodness and for fearing that your plan would lead us to misery.

Grant us the courage to lay our rebel hearts on the altar before you.

Teach us the joy of submission.

Bring us to the place where your will is our supreme desire.

Amen.

GOING DEEPER

1. Have you ever faced a moment so desperate that you felt you couldn't pray? Can you think of a time when you were afraid to pray "Your will be done," because you feared God's answer?

2. If you could ask the Lord one question about his will for your life, what would it be?

3. "When Christ calls, we have to go. We don't have to come back." What does that statement mean in your own life?

4. Read Matthew 26:36–45. When Jesus prayed in Gethsemane, what was the "cup" that he asked might be taken from him? What do we learn from Jesus' example about the cost of praying "your will be done"?

5. Is it true that God does not accept the status quo? In what sense is the prayer "Your will be done" an act of God-ordained rebellion against the evil of this world?

6. What happens to the person who refuses to pray "Your will be done?"

AN ACTION STEP

When you pray "Your will be done," you are asking that your life pass from your control to God's control. What are the signs that you are trying to control your own life? Circle the words that apply to you: irritable, pushy, anxious, fearful, hyperactive, withdrawn, driven, compulsive, critical, hypersensitive, perfectionistic, overbearing, worried. Spend some time asking God to set you free from the need always to be in control.

"Give us today our daily bread."
Matthew 6:11

CHAPTER SIX
DAILY BREAD LIVING

Before we begin: Name three things you pray about most often. Why does God want us to ask him to provide "daily" bread?

WITH THIS PETITION WE TURN A corner in our journey through the Lord's Prayer. The first three petitions direct our attention to God the Father. We are instructed to:

- Pray to the Father about his Name, "Hallowed be your name."
- Pray to the Father about his kingdom, "Your kingdom come."
- Pray to the Father about his will, "Your will be done."

The second half of the Lord's Prayer teaches us to pray for ourselves and for others. We are to:

- Pray for provision, "Give us today our daily bread."
- Pray for pardon, "Forgive us our debts."
- Pray for protection, "Lead us not into temptation."

A brief glance at the Lord's Prayer reveals that one word characterizes the first half of the prayer, and another word characterizes the second half of the prayer. The word for the first half is *your*—*your* name, *your* kingdom, *your* will. The word for the second half of the prayer is *us*—give *us,* forgive *us,* lead *us.* By arranging things this way, Jesus is teaching us that we are to begin with God's concerns. We are to pray to God about the things he is most concerned about. When we have done that, we are to pray for our own concerns—our daily bread, our forgiveness, and our protection in the moment of temptation. We start in heaven and then come down to earth, which is the pattern of all divine revelation.

GOD AND YOUR PROBLEMS

In the second half of this prayer, God is brought directly into the tiniest details of our everyday lives. If the first half of the prayer seems too esoteric, if the first half seems too theoretical, if it seems too theological—it shouldn't—but if for some reason it does, you will certainly understand and draw near to the second half of the Lord's Prayer, because it is meant for you and the problems you are facing in your daily life.

Let's take a look at the second half of the prayer and analyze it a little bit more. It contains three petitions: "give us our daily bread," "forgive us our debts," and "lead us not into temptation." That covers provision, pardon, and protection. If you think about those three things, they take care of all the needs of life:

- Provision takes care of your *present.*
- Pardon takes care of your *past.*
- Protection takes care of your *future.*

Not only that, but it also takes care of every part of you personally. Provision takes care of your *body.* Pardon takes care of your *soul.* Protection takes care of your *spirit.* Everything that can be brought legitimately into prayer is in the Lord's Prayer. That is why it is such a tragic mistake for us to overlook the Lord's Prayer or to think that it is just a Sunday morning ritual. It is more than just a pattern or model for prayer. If you understand it in its breadth, everything that you can legitimately pray about is contained in either the first half or the second half of this great prayer.

HOT BREAD FROM HEAVEN

Now we are ready to look at the second half of the prayer. It begins with a petition for provision: "Give us today our daily bread." We need to think about two words before we consider the deeper meaning of this petition. First, this is a prayer for bread, not for cake. "Give us today our daily *bread.*" The Greek word for *bread* refers to common, ordinary bread. It doesn't mean anything fancy. It just means normal, everyday bread. Jesus is telling us that when we pray, we ought to pray for ordinary, normal, everyday bread.

At its heart, this is a prayer for food. This is a prayer to be said before you sit down and eat. When was the last time you actually prayed to God, "O God, please give me a meal"? Most of us ought to pray the opposite, "O God, prevent me from eating another meal; I have already eaten too much." This petition sounds like it ought to be a prayer uttered by someone living in Haiti or Bangladesh. It's sad but true. We have so much food that we take this prayer request for granted, and yet this prayer request has formed a familiar childhood prayer:

> God is great.
> God is good.
> Let us thank him for our food.
> By his hands we all are fed.
> Give us Lord our daily bread.

But bread in Scripture is more than just literal bread; it's also a symbol for all the material needs of life. Bread in the Lord's Prayer stands not just for the kind of bread that you slice and eat. It also stands for all the physical and material needs of your life.

MARTIN LUTHER ON "DAILY BREAD"

In 1529, Martin Luther wrote his famous *Small Catechism* in which he explains the meaning of each part of the Apostles' Creed, the Ten Commandments, and the Lord's Prayer. This is what he says about "Give us today our daily bread":

> What does this mean? Truly, God gives daily bread to evil people, even without our prayer. But we pray in this request that he will help us realize this and receive our daily bread with thanksgiving.

> What does "Daily Bread" mean? Everything that nourishes our body and meets its needs, such as: Food, drink, clothing, shoes, house, yard, fields, cattle, money, possessions, a devout spouse, devout children, devout employees, devout and faithful rulers, good government, good weather, peace, health, discipline, honor, good friends, faithful neighbors and other things like these.[1]

The phrase "and other things like these" means anything he leaves out of the list, which means everything physical or material is contained in the expression "bread." You are not just praying for physical bread; you are praying for all the physical and material needs of life.

In the history of Bible interpretation, some people have been rather shocked that a prayer as exalted as the Lord's Prayer should contain a petition for something so mundane as daily bread. Over the centuries some commentators have suggested that daily bread represents something spiritual or sacred like the Lord's Supper. They were a little bit offended that something as earthy as daily bread and the needs of life would be in a great prayer like this. It seemed superfluous and even unspiritual to them. Try telling that to a starving man. If you haven't eaten in three days, the one thing you want more than anything else is daily bread. This petition is our invitation to earnestly ask God for the needs and necessities of life.

DAILY BREAD FOR DAILY NEEDS

The word *daily* also deserves our notice: "Give us today our *daily* bread." One commentator called it the only perplexing word in the whole Lord's Prayer. The Greek word is difficult because it appears only twice in the New Testament—in the two texts that contain the Lord's Prayer. And there aren't many examples of the word outside the New Testament.

So rare was this word that Origen (an early church father) suggested that perhaps Matthew and Luke coined this word to translate an Aramaic original for which there was no Greek equivalent. But a few years ago researchers found this word in an ancient fragment that appears to be a woman's grocery shopping list. She wrote down the things that she was going to buy when she went to the store, and next to certain items she wrote the Greek word translated "daily." In that context the word means either "buy it daily" or "buy it today." That clarifies the meaning of this word in the Lord's Prayer. It means "for this very day" or "for the day that is about to come."

If you pray this prayer in the morning, you are saying, "O God, may you give us today the material things that we need for today." If you pray this prayer at night, you are praying, "O God, may you give us tomorrow the things that we need for tomorrow."[2]

We can draw two conclusions from these two introductory points. *First, the fact that Jesus mentions bread teaches us that material things do not lie outside the realm of prayer.* Sometimes well-meaning people have thought that it is somehow unspiritual to pray for physical needs. That's not right. You're not just a soul or a spirit; you are a real person living in a real human body. If food is what you need, this prayer teaches you to pray for food. If money is what you need, this prayer teaches you to pray for money. If a job is what you need, this prayer teaches you to pray for a job. If health is what you need, this prayer teaches you to pray for health. If you need any physical thing, if it is legitimate, we have warrant here to bring it before God. Material things are not excluded from the realm of prayer.

Second, Jesus is teaching us the importance of moment-by-moment, 100 percent dependence on God for the things that we need. He's teaching us that we need to learn to depend on God on a day-to-day basis. As Matthew Henry said, this really means that the followers of Jesus Christ are to have "a hand to mouth existence."

With that as background, here is my thesis for this chapter. This great petition, "give us today our daily bread," is more than just a prayer request. Properly understood, it describes an entire way of looking at life. This petition suggests something about a truly Christian lifestyle. You could call it Daily Bread Living.

That is to say, if you are going to pray this prayer with understanding, it's going to lead to a certain attitude or a certain way of life. If this prayer is ever going to become reality, it must first affect the way you live. *Therefore I want to suggest four steps to Daily Bread Living.* Each step comes from the words of the text itself. These four steps to Daily Bread Living are really four qualities that need to be in your life if this prayer request is ever going to become a reality.

GRATITUDE

The first step to Daily Bread Living is gratitude to God for all his blessings. This step comes from the very first word. "*Give* us today our daily bread." This prayer request teaches us that everything we have comes from God. Everything. The clothes, the food, the friendships, the education, the mind we use, the words we speak, *everything* comes from God. We are put in the position of those who are praying, "O Heavenly Father, give us what we need." Surely this must be the central teaching—that gratitude to God is to mark our lives and we're to be grateful to God for all he's done.

Consider the words of Moses, "When you have eaten and are satisfied, praise the LORD your God for the good land he has given you" (Deut. 8:10). David says, "But who am I, and who are my people, that we should be able to give as generously as this? Everything comes from you, and we have given you only what comes from your hand" (1 Chron. 29:14). Again, David declares, "You open your hand and satisfy the desires of every living thing" (Ps. 145:16).

Have you ever stopped to think about the splendor of creation? God could have ordained that we eat nothing but mud. Mud for breakfast, mud for lunch, mud for supper. He could have made everything gray. But he didn't do that. He created a whole world for us, and he painted it in Technicolor. He said, "Here, eat and drink and be made strong. Everything I made, I put here for you." The whole world is yours to enjoy. Lying on the field looking up at the fleecy clouds. Letting the juice dribble down your cheeks when you're eating a luscious peach. Losing your breath when you jump into an ice-cold stream. Watching your grandchildren play at your feet. Climbing Horn Peak in Colorado. Listening at twilight to the "Goldberg Variations." All those things are gifts from Almighty God.

The animating principle of the Christian life is gratitude to God for all his blessings. Everything of value that you possess comes in one way or another from the hand of Almighty God. Everything you have at this moment, including the very breath you are breathing, comes as a gift of the Father. This truth ought to make us grateful for the gift of life itself.

Recently I happened to catch a few minutes of an interview with Hamilton Jordan, chief of staff under President Jimmy Carter. He has written a book with the intriguing title, *No Such Thing as a Bad Day.* It's his own story about being diagnosed with cancer on three separate occasions before the age of fifty. "Where did the title come from?" asked the interviewer. Hamilton Jordan said he called a friend with cancer who is also a father with several young children. After they chatted for a bit, Mr. Jordan asked him, "Are you having a bad day?" "When the doctors tell you that you have only three months to live, there is no such thing as a bad day," the man replied.

What a world of truth lies in those simple words. If you know you're only going to live for a few weeks, every day becomes precious, and you simply don't have time to have a "bad day." You get up every morning, smell the roses, and drink deeply of the elixir called life. Even the moments of sadness are there to be savored and remembered, because soon those moments will be gone. I think Mr. Jordan's point is that in some strange way what happened to that young father was a gift from God. Not the dying part, because that is heartbreaking to contemplate. But the other part, the realization that since you won't be here long you simply don't have time to dwell on the negative. You see the sand slipping from the hourglass, and you choose and choose again to make every moment count.

How different this is from the way most of us live. We can afford to have "bad days," because we're planning on living a long time. A "bad day" is a luxury we give ourselves because we figure with so many more years to go, we can pout or be miserable or have a pity party or feel sorry for ourselves today. The dying have no such luxury. Only the living dare to go into the corner and sulk. Years ago I heard someone say that happiness is a choice. All the virtues and all the vices are choices we make. Happiness is a choice. So is anger. And gratitude. And kindness. And sloth. And patience. And doubt. And faith. We are the way we are because we choose to be that way. And we stay the way we are because we choose not to change.

"So teach us to number our days," said the psalmist, "that we may apply our hearts unto wisdom" (Ps. 90:12 KJV). How true. Life is too short to have a bad day.

HE JUST JUMPS RIGHT IN

Harry Ironside tells of the occasion when, as a young man, he went into a cafeteria to eat. The tables were crowded, and the only place he could find to sit down was at a table across from another man. So he sat down, and as was his habit, Ironside bowed his head and gave thanks.

The other man glowered while he did so, and as soon as Ironside had finished, the man looked at him and said, "What's the matter with you. Is something wrong with your food?"

He looked down at it and said, "No, it looks fine to me."

The fellow said, "Have you got something in your eye? Do you have a headache?"

Ironside said, "No, I'm feeling fine."

The fellow said, "What are you doing then? Why did you bow your head?"

Ironside said, "Well, I was just giving thanks to God for the food I was about to eat."

The man looked at him and said, "You believe that stuff, do you? That's crazy."

Ironside said, "Sir, don't you give thanks for your food?"

The man said, "I never give thanks. I just jump right in."

Ironside looked at him and said, "Well, you're just like my dog then. He doesn't give thanks either. He just jumps right in."[3]

The lesson is not about praying before a meal. The lesson is about being truly grateful to God for all of his blessings. There are basically two ways you can live your life. You can live your life with a big *M* and a little *g* or a big G and a little *m*.

BIG GOD	little God
little me	BIG ME

The first step to Daily Bread Living is to get on the big G and the little *m* side. That's gratitude to God for all his blessings.

CONTENTMENT

The second step to Daily Bread Living is *contentment with what God has already provided.* The key to the second step is in the last word: "Give us today our daily *bread.*" We are invited to ask for bread, not for cake. We are to pray, "Give us today our daily bread," not "our daily dessert." Jesus encourages us to pray to

God for our *needs,* not for our *greeds.* The way a pauper will pray this prayer will differ from the way a prince will pray this prayer. But the principle is the same. We are to pray and ask God for what we really *need,* not for every wild desire that comes into our mind. This prayer is not an invitation to pray for great material wealth simply so we can add to our bottom line. Nor is it an invitation to pray for everything in the latest Christmas catalogue. Not that those things are wrong in themselves. But the text says "bread," not "chocolate eclair." We are to trust God for the things we really need.

WHEN JESUS DOES THE COOKING

Have you ever studied the way Jesus ate? What you find is revealing. First, Jesus enjoyed good food. Jesus repeatedly went to festivals and feasts and to rich and sumptuous banquets. He went so often that the Pharisees called him a glutton and a drunkard. Our Lord enjoyed good food. He felt at home among the wealthy of the world. But whenever Jesus did the cooking, things were different. Basically there was one menu—baked fish and barley bread. Our Lord Jesus could enjoy as a gift the good things of the world, but when he himself did the cooking, it was simple and nutritious. Our Lord Jesus was truly comfortable with the high and mighty and the wealthy, and he did not mind eating their food; but when he did the cooking, the menu changed dramatically.

I traveled to Russia not long after the fall of Communism. Upon my return to America, many people wanted to know about the food. I never ate better in my life. It seemed like we had three or four meals every day. Wherever we went, we enjoyed the hospitality of Russian believers. The average Russian family has much less than most Americans have of this world's goods, and yet when you go there, they open the cupboards wide, and they keep bringing it out.

During my visit I was greatly blessed by a particular custom we followed in almost every home. At the beginning of the meal, we all stood and bowed our heads and thanked God for the food. Then we sat down and shared our meal together. At the end of the meal, we stood up again and we prayed, thanking God for what we had just received. That made a powerful impact on my life. That is what Jesus is talking about. That's what it means to say that God has given you daily bread—to be truly thankful and truly content with what he has provided.

Many of us need to ponder the words of Proverbs 30:7–9: "Two things I ask of you, O LORD; do not refuse me before I die: Keep falsehood and lies far from me; give me neither poverty nor riches, but give me only my daily bread. Otherwise, I may have too much and disown you and say, 'Who is the LORD?' Or I may become poor and steal, and so dishonor the name of my God."

What a wonderful outlook on life. "Lord, don't make me too rich or too poor. O God, give me whatever you think is enough, and I will be content."

CONFIDENCE

The third step to Daily Bread Living is *confidence that God will meet my needs day by day.* You can find this principle in two places in our text: "Give us today our daily bread." Daily Bread Living means believing that God will provide what you need on a day-by-day basis. The experience of the children of Israel in the Sinai wilderness provides a powerful illustration of this principle. Exodus 16 records the story. The children of Israel had just crossed the Red Sea. After that great miracle, they started grumbling. Now they're out in the middle of the desert, and they're saying, "Why did you bring us out here? At least we got to eat back in Egypt. Who cares about miracles? We're going to starve to death."

So Moses went to God and said, "God, I've got trouble with your people."

And God said, "Tell them to get ready because I am going to provide food for them. So the Lord sent the children of Israel manna and quail. The quail were going to come flying in low to the ground at night. The next morning the Jews would find dew on the ground and when the dew disappeared, they would find wafers that tasted like crackers with honey. Manna.

God's instructions were specific: "Go out and get as much as you need for yourself and your family. But don't get any more than you need. Why? Because if you get any more than you need, it will rot and the maggots will infest your quail. On the day before the Sabbath, you can collect for two days, but that's it. Anyone who tries to hoard extra manna will end up with a worm-infested, rotting mess."

I'm sure if I had been there, I would have sent my three sons out with the wheelbarrow that first week and told them, "Put some under the bed. You never know; this may not show up tomorrow." I think I would have been on the wormy side of things for a couple of weeks just trying to play it safe.

God is teaching us in the Old Testament the same thing he is trying to teach us in the New Testament. *He is willing to supply our needs but only on a day-to-day basis.* We don't like to live like that. Most of us have freezers at home filled with food. Maybe we have a side of beef and some vegetables. We have plenty of food. There is nothing wrong with that, by the way, but a freezer filled with food makes it more challenging to pray this prayer sincerely. We mutter our prayers instead of saying them from the heart, because we already know we aren't going to go hungry.

We don't like to live the way Jesus is talking about here. We don't want to live day to day. We'd rather have pension plans and stocks and bonds and options. We would rather have life insurance policies that guarantee a secure future. If we had our way, this prayer would read, "Give us this week our weekly bread." Or, "Give us this month our monthly bread." Or better yet, "Lord, give us this year our yearly bread. Just give it to us all at once, and we'll be all right. Then we'll trust you."

God does not work that way. He works by teaching his people moment-by-moment dependence on him.

INCREASING UNCERTAINTY

Life *is* uncertain. Most of us don't have enough savings to get through another month. You can be doing fine, and then one day the doctor says, "I'm sorry. The tests are positive. You've got cancer." Your life gets rearranged in a split second. Just when you think you've got it all together, an illness, the loss of a job, the collapse of an empire that you put together, can happen so fast. One reason God lets those things happen is to move us away from self-sufficiency to God-sufficiency. From self-reliance to God-reliance. From trusting in our own ability to trusting in him alone.

Not long ago I talked with one of the single mothers of our congregation who owns her own business. "How's it going?"

She smiled and said, "We're barely making it. June was tough. But I've got two jobs for July. We're going to be OK for July. That's the way it is. Just when we're about to run out, God brings in a little more work." That's not easy, but that dear woman has discovered something that those of us who have plenty of money never discover. She's discovering that God *will* meet her needs.

Does this mean that we shouldn't plan ahead? Not at all. You should plan ahead. That's biblical. You should plan ahead, but you shouldn't *worry ahead*. There's a big difference. The whole point of asking for *daily* bread is to teach us to take life one day at a time. Men and women who are in a twelve-step program already know that. It's a basic principle for healing of the inner life: You can get better, but you must take it one day at a time. You don't get better a week at a time or a month at a time. You get better one day at a time. That is a tremendous principle. Daily Bread Living means taking life one day at a time and being confident that God will take care of your needs day by day.

GENEROSITY

The fourth step to Daily Bread Living is *generosity toward those who are less fortunate.* This principle comes from the little word *our.* "Give us today *our* daily bread." It does not say, "Give me *my* daily bread." That's a completely different prayer. You're never invited to pray for yourself alone. Every time you pray this prayer you are invited and encouraged and even commanded to pray in concert with your brothers and sisters. We all eat from the same table. This petition imparts a bigness, a vastness, a broadness to your prayers. It takes you out of the narrow focus of your own problems, and it opens you up to a whole world of people all around you.

This thought runs against the grain of modern society. In the marketplace only the tough survive. You've got to look out for yourself and make sure no one is gaining on you. It's a dog-eat-dog world out there. Whoever works the hardest gets the most. The world says, "Get to the top any way you can." How different that is from the words of Jesus, "Give, and it shall be given unto you" (Luke 6:38 KJV). It is a jungle out there, and the business world runs by the law of the jungle. Only the tough survive. You've got to look out for number one. It is open warfare, and you have to be willing to do what it takes to get to the top. It's totally opposite of what Jesus is suggesting here.

BIBLICAL ECONOMICS 101

Here are four principles that underlie the call to share with those who have less than you do:

- Principle 1: *Everything you have comes from God.*

- Principle 2: *Everything that is given to you is given in trust to you.*
- Principle 3: *The blessings that you have are not given to you for your own personal benefit.*
- Principle 4: *What is given to you in trust is given that you might share it with others.*

What you have is not simply to be used for yourself; it is to be used for the benefit of others. You might call this Biblical Economics 101. *What you have is loaned to you that you might give it to other people.* To say "*our* daily bread" is to see a world of needy and hurting people. *Our* implies that you don't pray alone. To say *our,* instead of *my* or *mine,* imparts a liberality to your prayer. This is liberality, not charity; benevolence, not welfare. Most of us will have all we want to eat today, and tomorrow we'll have all we want, and the day after that and the day after that. Yet our world is filled with starving people. When we pray "Give us today our daily bread," we can never pray as if we were the only people in the world. We are to pray thinking about the needy around us. And if we're not thinking about the needy around us, we ought not to pray this prayer at all.

When the rich man prays, he will also pray for wretched Lazarus at the gate. And if the rich man's prayer is sincere, he's going to make sure that Lazarus has more than mere crumbs to eat. If God has given you two loaves of bread and your brother has only one, that extra loaf is not for storing. It's for sharing. That's what this prayer is about. That's the fourth step to Daily Bread Living.

A PLACE TO BEGIN

This petition, like all the others, opens us up into a whole new way of looking at life. It's far more than just a few words on a piece of paper. This is what the Christian life is all about. So what is Daily Bread Living? Let me summarize. Daily Bread Living is:

1. Gratitude to God for all of his blessings.
2. Contentment with what God has already given you.
3. Confidence that God will meet your needs day by day.
4. Generosity toward those who are less fortunate than you.

Gratitude. Contentment. Confidence. Generosity. That's what Daily Bread Living is all about. If you pray this prayer enough, that's where you'll end up. It's not a bad place to be.

BOB AND AMBER'S EXCELLENT ADVENTURE

This petition reminds us that God delights to hear our prayers, even when we are praying for things that seem small or mundane or "not important enough" to bother God. For most of us, the real challenge is learning to lay every part of life before the Lord.

Bob and Amber Leland stopped by to see me one final time before leaving the Chicago area to return to Irian Jaya for another term of missionary service. When we got together, Bob had something definite on his mind. He took out some sheets of paper and said he wanted to check on the answers to some prayer requests. There must have been almost fifty different items covering many different areas of our church life. Each one had been written down and the date noted. Some were labeled "continual," and others were for specific needs.

We went over each request one by one. Bob asked me to tell him if the request had been answered. He would write down *yes, no,* or *not yet,* depending on what I said. Some of the requests were for things such as revival in the congregation and spiritual power in the preaching of God's Word. Others were particular, such as additional workers for our children's ministry. On and on we went, covering the church, the staff, and also Oak Park Christian Academy. Some of the requests went back four or five years. I marveled as I thought about the faithfulness of these two servants of Christ laboring in prayer from the Bird's Head coastline of Irian Jaya.

I asked Bob when he and Amber started writing down prayer requests and noting the answers. He told me they started in 1971 because "we were bored with our prayer life. It seemed like we prayed and prayed but never heard about any answers." So thirty years ago they began writing down specific requests. Whenever they agreed to pray for something or someone, they decided to go back later and find out how God had answered their prayers. And that's why they had come to my office for one final visit. They wanted to know what God had done through their prayers. Bob told me that after three decades of doing this, they have discovered that approximately 89 percent of their prayers are answered yes, 2 percent are answered no, and about 9 percent are answered not yet. "It's hard to argue with that," he said with a smile. Bob is right. It is hard to argue with that.

KEEPING TRACK OF GOD'S ANSWERS

I hesitate to share their story because it can so easily be misused. Some people may think that prayer is like playing some giant slot machine in the sky. And others may think it is unspiritual to tally the answers to your prayers. I don't think the percentage matters, but I do think Bob and Amber Leland have found a practical solution to the problem of boredom in prayer. They simply keep track of God's answers. That is certainly biblical. The percentages just make the story memorable.

Why have so many of their prayers been answered? I think it's because Bob and Amber have dedicated themselves to knowing and doing the will of God. As they have delighted themselves in the Lord, his desires have become part of their desires so that when they pray, they are truly praying according to God's will. Why should we be surprised when God answers our prayers when we pray in his will? Should we not expect God to keep his Word? Perhaps we would all benefit by keeping a record of our prayers and God's answers. Certainly this is in the spirit of Jesus who said, "Keep asking, and it will be given to you" (Matt. 7:7 HCSB).

The converted slave-trader John Newton expressed this truth in these words from an old hymn:

> Thou art coming to a King,
> Large petitions with thee bring;
> For His grace and power are such,
> None can ever ask too much.

GIVING IN, GIVING UP, OR GIVING THANKS

A. W. Tozer once remarked that "a thankful heart cannot be cynical." I paused when I read that because we certainly live in a cynical age. The cynic is a person who, having seen the bad side of human nature so often, finds it hard to take anything at face value. On one hand, such a person can be refreshingly realistic compared to the pie-in-the-sky dreamers who never question anything. The famous axiom of the newspaper reporter comes to mind: "If your mother says she loves you, check it out." Well, it's good to check out things and to have a healthy dose of skepticism when the voice on the phone offers you a "free" trip to Hawaii if you'll just listen to a one-hour sales presentation—no pressure, of course.

But that's not the whole story. A little cynicism can be positive, but like any virtue it can quickly become a vice. The heart of gratitude comes from realizing that God alone is the source of all our blessings. Everything else is derivative. I have what I have because God has willed me to have it. I live where I live because God has willed me to live here. I was born into a particular family because God willed it to be so. I was born in Tennessee, raised in Alabama, met my wife in Chattanooga, went to seminary in Dallas, and now live in Oak Park because God has willed it so. And even my problems (which aren't many) are apportioned to me by the hand of a loving God.

Life is a journey with many twists and turns, and as I creep toward my fiftieth birthday—just a few months from now—I find that I believe in the sovereignty of God more than ever before. That means there is no such thing as luck or fate or chance. This includes the trivial details of life and the things that really matter like life and death, health and sickness, and what the future holds for our loved ones. I heard about a little girl who, when asked what she had learned in Sunday school, said that she had learned that "God never says, 'Oops.'" That's comforting to know because we live in an "Oops!" world where mistakes are made all the time, often by well-meaning people.

The true cynic doubts that God knows or cares, and he therefore gives in to doubt, anger, and sometimes to utter despair. But those who know their God know that he knows even when they don't know, and instead of giving in or giving up, they give thanks. It is this spirit that causes us to ask God for the daily bread we need and then to trust that he will answer this prayer every time, day after day, in his own way, according to his own will.

GOING DEEPER

1. When, if ever, have you sincerely prayed for God to provide food so you would have something to eat?

2. Psalm 105 is a poetic retelling of God's deliverance of the Jews from Egypt. From this psalm, name the various ways in which God supplied "daily bread" for his people.

3. "The followers of Jesus Christ are to have a 'hand to mouth' existence." What does this statement mean? Do you agree or disagree? How does this relate to saving money, building your investments, and amassing personal wealth?

4. What does the story of God's provision of manna and quail (Exod. 16) teach us about the way God supplies our needs?

PRAYER

Gracious Father,

Teach us to trust you more and more.

When we are tempted to do it ourselves, bring us down to the place where we must cry out for your help.

Forgive us for living as if we were God and you are not.

We thank you for giving us exactly what we need, when we need it, not a moment too soon, and not moment too late.

Having received so much from you, we ask one thing more. Give us grateful hearts.

Amen.

5. Would your friends consider you a grateful person? Why or why not?

6. Why can a cynical person not be thankful? And how can a grateful heart cure a cynical spirit?

A TRUTH TO REMEMBER:
Daily Bread Living means believing that because God is God, he will give you what you truly need when you truly need it.

AN ACTION STEP

Most of us like to make lists. We make lists of things to do, people to see, projects to complete, and so on. Take your to-do list this week and turn it into a prayer list. Instead of becoming stressed out about all the things you have to do in the next few days, bring your to-do list to the Lord and say, "Lord, this is beyond me—beyond my strength, beyond my wisdom, beyond my power. Lord, I'm bringing it to you and asking you to strengthen me and help me." Keep a record during the next week of how God answers your prayers.

"Forgive us our debts, as we also have forgiven our debtors."
MATTHEW 6:12

CHAPTER SEVEN

UNLESS YOU FORGIVE

Before we begin: Which is more difficult for you: asking God to forgive you or forgiving a person who has sinned against you?

THE FIFTH PETITION OF THE LORD'S Prayer seems simple enough, but simple things can sometimes be deep. These are the words of Jesus: "Forgive us our debts, as we also have forgiven our debtors." Everyone agrees that this is a difficult word from the Lord. It is hard to understand and even harder to apply. Our basic problem is simple: The Lord has apparently drawn something into this prayer that does not belong there. We would understand this petition perfectly if it read, "Forgive us our debts," and just stopped right there. That would make sense. We all understand that we need to confess our sins and ask for forgiveness. We know that confession and repentance are part of what prayer is all about.

What makes this prayer so frustrating is that Jesus seems to drag in something that doesn't belong when he adds the phrase "as we also have forgiven our debtors." At first glance, there doesn't seem to be any necessary connection between the first part of the petition and the second part.

GRACE OR WORKS?

It seems as if Jesus is saying, "The way you treat other people is the way God will treat you." On one level that thought is puzzling; on another it is profoundly disquieting. On still another level it appears to present a major theological difficulty. Not long ago I was invited to appear before our high school youth group for an event called Stump the Pastor. The teenagers were asked to write their questions ahead of time, and they were encouraged to be both creative and obscure. Several of the students excelled in the latter category by asking things like "Who or what was Ziv?" and "Who is listed as the seventh-to-the-last ancestor of Joseph?" But one question dealt with this petition. It went something like this: "Why does Jesus say that we should pray to be forgiven as we forgive others? Why would Almighty God tie himself to what we do on earth?" I think that's a good question.

So this petition is puzzling, difficult, and one that bothers every sincere thinker. It makes you wonder what Jesus really meant. Is Jesus here teaching that God's forgiveness is conditional? Is he teaching us that our forgiveness with God is somehow predicated on *our* forgiving other people? It would appear at first reading that that is indeed what he is teaching. If so, is this not teaching us that forgiveness is a work by which we gain God's favor? What then happens to the great biblical doctrine of the grace of God? When it comes to forgiveness, who takes the first step—God or man?

Indeed, this is a difficult text. Because it is difficult, let me state my conclusion at the beginning of this chapter. This verse means exactly what it says. The teaching of this verse can be given in one simple sentence: *Unless you forgive, God will not forgive you.* Nothing is hidden here; nothing is tricky. Jesus *is* saying that unless you forgive, you will not be forgiven.

SIGNING YOUR OWN DEATH WARRANT

Augustine called this text "a terrible petition." He pointed out that if you pray these words while harboring an unforgiving spirit, you are actually asking God not to forgive you. Ponder that for a moment. If you pray, "Forgive us our debts, as we also have forgiven our debtors," while refusing to forgive those who have wronged you, this prayer—which is meant to be a blessing—becomes a self-inflicted curse. In that case you are really saying, "O God, since I have not forgiven my brother, please do not forgive me." That is why Charles Haddon Spurgeon, the great English preacher, said that if you pray the Lord's Prayer with an unforgiving spirit, you have virtually signed your own death warrant.

During one period of his life, John Wesley was a missionary in the American colonies—primarily in the area that would become the state of Georgia. Wesley had some dealings with a general by the name of Oglethorpe. General Oglethorpe was a great military leader, but he had a reputation as a harsh and brutal man. One day he said to John Wesley, "I never forgive." To which Wesley replied, "Then, sir, I hope you never sin."

THE KEY WORD

When we pray, "Forgive us our debts, as we also have forgiven our debtors," we are asking God to forgive our sins according to the same standard we have used in forgiving the sins of others. There are eleven words in the text, but only one of them is important for our purposes. It's the little word *as.* Everything hangs on the meaning of that word. *As* is the conjunction that joins the first half of the petition with the second half.

When Jesus says "as," he is setting up a comparison between the way we forgive and the way God forgives us. This text says that we set the standard, and then God follows the standard. We establish the pattern, and then God follows that pattern in the way he deals with us.

When you pray this prayer, you are really saying, "O God, deal with me as I deal with other people. Deal with me as I have dealt with others." We are virtually saying, "O God, I've got a neighbor, and I did some favors for my neighbor, and my neighbor is ungrateful to me for all I have done. I am angry at my neighbor, and I will not forgive him for his ingratitude. Now deal with me as I have dealt with my neighbor." It's as if we're praying, "O God, that man hurt me. I am so angry I can't wait to get even. Deal with me as I have dealt with him." We set the standard, and God follows our lead.

NO EXCEPTIONS

Unless you forgive, you will not be forgiven. These are the words of C. S. Lewis:

> No part of his teaching is clearer: And there are no exceptions to it. He doesn't say that we are to forgive other people's sins providing they are not too frightful, or providing there are extenuating circumstances, or anything of that sort. We are to forgive them all, however spiteful, however mean, however often they are repeated. If we don't, we shall be forgiven none of our own.[1]

To refuse to forgive someone else and then to ask God for forgiveness is a kind of spiritual schizophrenia. You are asking God to give you what you are unwilling to give to someone else. The fifth petition of the Lord's Prayer tells us you cannot have it both ways. Do you want to be forgiven? You must forgive others. Unless you forgive, you will not be forgiven.

A SERIOUS WORD TO THE UNFORGIVING

But does the Bible really teach that God's forgiveness of us is somehow linked to our forgiveness of others? Yes, indeed it does. Let's go back to the words of Jesus, the fifth petition is in verse 12. Now drop down two verses. The Lord's Prayer is over, but Jesus is still speaking. "For if you forgive men when they sin against you, your heavenly Father will also forgive you. But if you do not forgive men their sins, your Father will not forgive your sins" (Matt. 6:14–15).

I call one crucial fact to your attention: Jesus has just given us the Lord's Prayer, and the only part that he singles out for additional commentary is the fifth petition. All the others he leaves alone. I believe he offered further commentary because he knew that we would feel uncomfortable with this part of the Lord's Prayer. He knew that we would try to wiggle out from under it. That is why in verses 14–15 he spells it out so clearly that no one can doubt it.

THE UNFORGIVING SERVANT

In case you doubt what I am saying, consider the story Jesus told in Matthew 18:21–35. "Then Peter came to Him and said, 'Lord, how many times could my brother sin against me and I forgive him? As many as seven times?' 'I tell you, not as many as seven,' Jesus said to him, 'but seventy times seven'" (vv. 21–22 HCSB).

That's 490 times. The clunk you just heard is Peter dropping over in a dead faint. He can't believe his ears. Then Jesus went on to give a parable.

> "For this reason, the kingdom of heaven can be compared to a king who wanted to settle accounts with his slaves. When he began to settle accounts, one who owed ten thousand talents was brought before him. Since he had no way to pay it back, his master commanded that he, his wife, his children, and everything he had be sold to pay the debt.

> "At this, the slave fell down on his face before him and said, 'Be patient with me, and I will pay you everything!' Then the master of that slave had compassion, released him, and forgave him the load" (vv. 23–27 HCSB).

Once upon a time there was a great king who ruled a vast realm. He was a man of extraordinary wealth—perhaps the richest person in the entire world. He had a steward—a man who worked for him, a man who was in charge of his entire legal and financial affairs. The king said to the steward, "Take care of everything for me." And the king went about his affairs, leaving everything in the hands of his servant. Evidently the king didn't pay very close attention to what his servant was doing. While the king was otherwise occupied, his servant ran up a debt of ten thousand talents, which would be like twenty-five million dollars. How did he run up a tab of twenty-five million? We don't know how he did it, but he may have been running some sort of tax scam where he overcharged for taxes and kept the overage for himself.

At length the day came when the king wanted an accounting. His CPAs ran the numbers, called the man in before the king, and delivered the bad news. "Your Majesty, this man owes you twenty-five million dollars." When the king asks, "How much money do you have?" the man answers, "I'm sorry, O King, but I'm broke." That's the second amazing fact of the story. First, he runs up his huge debt totally undetected, and then somehow he manages to spend it all. Wasn't anyone paying attention? Not only did he steal that much money, but he also spent that much money. He is both iniquitous and stupid. This man doesn't have anything with which to pay back the great debt to the king.

So the king says, "You are going to have to pay me back." The man falls on his knees and begs for mercy. He says something that again proves his stupidity, "Your Highness, give me time, and I will pay back everything I owe you." That's crazy. He couldn't pay back what he owed in twenty lifetimes. But something moved the heart of the king to mercy and compassion. The Bible says that the king forgave the man the twenty-five million-dollar debt when he could have punished him. Forgave him when he could have thrown him in jail. Forgave him when he could have had his life. He forgave him, and this man who owed everything got up and walked away a free man. His debt had been wiped away.

But that's not the end of the story. "But that slave went out and found one of his fellow slaves who owed him a hundred denarii. [A hundred denarii would be like owing five thousand dollars compared to twenty-five million dollars. It's a relatively small amount of money.] He grabbed him, started choking him, and said, 'Pay what you owe!' At this, his fellow slave fell down and began begging him, 'Be patient with me, and I will pay you back'" (vv. 28–29 HCSB).

Verse 29 is an exact replay of verse 26. This poor fellow who owes five thousand dollars begs for mercy, using exactly the same words the first servant had used before the king.

"But he wasn't willing. On the contrary, he went and threw him into prison until he could pay what was owed. When the other slaves saw what had taken place, they were deeply distressed and went and reported to their master everything that had happened. Then, after he had summoned him, his master said to him, 'You wicked slave! I forgave you all that debt because you begged me. Shouldn't you also have had mercy on your fellow slave, as I had mercy on you?'" (vv. 30–33 HCSB).

That last phrase is really the point of this whole story. "Shouldn't you have had mercy on him just as I had on you?" The answer, of course, is yes. The shocking thing was not that this man wanted the five-thousand-dollar debt paid back. The shocking thing was that he was so unforgiving after having received such great mercy himself. What the king is saying is, "I forgave your twenty-five million-dollar debt; couldn't you have forgiven a measly five-thousand-dollar debt?"

This time the king is not going to be calm, and he is not going to be conned a second time. This time the king is not going to believe some sob story. Verse 34 says, "And his master got angry and handed him over to the jailers until he could pay everything that was owed" (HCSB). The moral of the story is in verse 35. "So my heavenly Father will also do to you if each of you does not forgive his brother from his heart" (HCSB). Please note. These words are for Christians. This is a warning to genuine believers concerning what will happen to them if they refuse to forgive.

THE HIDDEN TORTURERS

In order to understand the full impact of this story, consider this question: *Whose forgiveness came first? Answer: The king's forgiveness came first. It's in light of his great forgiveness that this servant's unforgiving spirit is such a terrible thing.* The king in the story is God, and you and I are like that unforgiving servant. We're called in before Almighty God, and when the story of our lives is read, there is a mountain of debt between God and us. It's so high we can't get over it, so wide we can't get around it, so deep we can't crawl under it.

So we fall on our knees and cry out to God, "O God, have mercy on me, have mercy on me for Jesus' sake." God looks down at us and he says, "You don't deserve it, but for Jesus' sake I will forgive you." In one great moment of grace that mountain of debt is swept away, and we rise, walk out of church singing to ourselves, "Lord, we lift your name on high." And just as we are going out to the parking lot, we see somebody who has sinned against us. Suddenly the joy disappears, and we want to go over and grab them and choke them and say, "Pay me what you owe me."

No wonder we're so unhappy. No wonder we're so frustrated. No wonder we can't sleep at night. No wonder we have ulcers and back pains and headaches and all kinds of illnesses that come to us. No wonder we carry grudges. No wonder we are depressed and confused. It has happened to us exactly as Jesus said. *We suffer because we who have been forgiven have harbored an unforgiving spirit.* Jesus said, "When my children refuse to forgive others, I hand them over to the torturers who will torture them day and night until they learn to forgive from the heart." What torturers? The hidden torturers of anger and bitterness that eat your insides out; the torturers of frustration and malice that give you ulcers and high blood pressure and migraine headaches; the torturers that make you lie awake at night stewing over every rotten thing that happens to you; the hidden torturers of an unforgiving heart who stalk your trail day and night, who never leave your side, who suck every bit of joy from your heart.

Why? Because you will not forgive from the heart.

TWO OBJECTIONS

Two objections are often raised to the teaching I have just given. The first objection relates to the first half of the petition, and the second one relates to the second half. *First, some people say that Christians should never have to confess their sins.* They argue that in light of our standing in Jesus Christ, we should never have to confess our sins and ask for forgiveness. They point out that justification means all of our sins have been forgiven—past, present, and future.

That's true, by the way, and I do not doubt that the Bible teaches it (Rom. 5:1). But I do not believe it is correct to infer from the fact of our justification that we should never ask for forgiveness. Those who hold this view suggest that confessing your sins to God will make you introspective and negative. They imply that to confess your sins is virtually to doubt God's work in your life. I have only one answer. Jesus said we were to pray, "Forgive us our debts." Period. Jesus said we were to do it. That overrules all theological objections. If Jesus said we are to do it, then that's what we have to do.

But what about the apparent contradiction between our position in Christ and the need to ask God for daily forgiveness? John R. Rice has the following helpful comment on this point:

> Though all my trespasses are already forgiven me (Col. 2:13) and not one of them can ever be charged against me to the condemnation of my soul, yet God is displeased when I sin and sin interferes with the communion of the child with his "Father which is in heaven." Referring to the salvation of my soul, my sins are already all forgiven. But when fresh sin comes between the happy fellowship of the Father and child, then that sin needs to be removed, that is, forgiven, in the secondary sense. . . . And this daily cleansing and daily restoration of intimate, sweet fellowship with the Father we cannot have unless we forgive others their sins against us![2]

Jesus said in this prayer that we are to pray that our sins might be forgiven. That much is clear. In Jesus Christ all your sins—past, present, and future—are forgiven. Is there a contradiction here? No, not at all. *When Jesus says we should pray, "Forgive us our debts," justification is not in view.* He is speaking to his own disciples, to those who are already justified. This petition is not for unbelievers; it is for believers who have already been justified. It is the already justified who are told to pray, "Forgive us our debts."

Jesus is teaching us that day by day as we sin we need to confess our sins, and we need to be forgiven of our sins day by day. On the night before his crucifixion, Jesus washed the disciples' feet in the upper room (John 13:1–17). When Peter's turn came, he told Jesus not to stop with his feet but to wash his head and hands as well. Jesus replied with words that speak to this issue:

"One who has bathed doesn't need to wash anything except his feet, but he is completely clean. You are clean" (John 13:10 HCSB). The body itself was clean from the earlier bath, but the feet are dirty from the dust of the day. When there is daily sin (the dust on the feet), there needs to be daily cleansing at the hands of the Lord Jesus Christ. Whenever you think about Matthew 6:12, you should also remember 1 John 1:9—a verse written to believers: "If we confess our sins, he is faithful and just to forgive us our sins, and to cleanse us from all unrighteousness" (KJV).

IS GOD'S FORGIVENESS CONDITIONAL?

A second objection is sometimes raised against this teaching. This objection is more serious, in my opinion. Is Jesus teaching us that God's forgiveness is conditional? In one sense (and only in one limited sense), the answer is yes. I know of no other way to read this passage of Scripture. But we must carefully qualify this teaching. Remember, the Lord's Prayer is not given to unbelievers but to believers. It's given to those who have already been forgiven by God. It's given to people who have experienced the grace of God. You've got to put Matthew 6 with Matthew 18 to get the right interpretation. There is no contradiction between those two passages. In the parable of Matthew 18, the king's forgiveness comes first. *Forgiveness always begins with God.*

Ephesians 4:32 says it plainly: "Be kind and compassionate to one another, forgiving one another, just as God also forgave you in Christ" (HCSB). That's past tense. Forgiveness begins with God. It never begins with us. Every blessing we receive—

salvation, forgiveness, justification, the new birth, new life in the Christ, the indwelling of the Holy Spirit, to name only a few—starts with God and comes down to us. God is the giver, and we are always on the receiving end of what he gives.

Now go back to the parable. We represent that servant whose great debts had already been forgiven in the past. It's on that basis that the Lord gives these verses in Matthew 6. There is no contradiction whatsoever. Let me say it plainly: Matthew 6 assumes the prior forgiveness of God that is clearly expressed in Matthew 18. Jesus is *not* teaching two different ways of forgiveness. There is always only one way of forgiveness. God is always the *source* of forgiveness. The blood of Christ is always the *ground* of forgiveness. A repentant heart is always the *condition* of forgiveness. A forgiving spirit is always the *evidence* of forgiveness. The removal of sin and restoration of fellowship is always the *result* of forgiveness.

John Walvoord explains Matthew 6:12 this way:

> Forgiveness is sought, assuming that the petitioner also forgives, although the reverse order is observed in the epistles; that is, we should forgive because we are forgiven. In the family relationship the other aspect is also true. The Christian already forgiven judicially should not expect restoration in the family relationship unless he, himself, is forgiving. Verse 12 does not deal with salvation but the relationship of a child to his father.[3]

There is no contradiction between Matthew 6 and Matthew 18. Both passages teach the same truth, only from different points of view. God's forgiveness comes first. It establishes our position in Christ and removes the judicial punishment for our sin. On the basis of God's forgiveness, we are called to forgive others. If we refuse to forgive as we have already been forgiven (at the moment we trusted Christ), we will not be forgiven (in terms of the moment-by-moment cleansing we need to maintain intimate fellowship with God).

AN "UNFORGIVEN" CHRISTIAN

What happens when a believer holds a grudge? What happens when he refuses to forgive? What happens when a Christian harbors anger and ill feelings toward those who have wronged him? Is he forgiven? Yes, in the sense that he is justified before God. Yes, in the sense that when he dies, he will go to heaven. No, he is not forgiven in the sense of having daily cleansing and sweet fellowship with the Lord. He is "in Christ" and "out of fellowship" with the Lord. He is walking in the flesh. He has given Satan a foothold in his life (cf. Eph. 4:26–27). He is walking in disobedience before the Lord. And he opens himself up to divine chastisement by the Lord (see Heb. 12:4–11). "Unconfessed sin leads to a state of disagreement. You may be God's child, but you don't want to talk to him." Until you make things right by forgiving those who have sinned against you, things will never be right between you and the Lord.[4]

As strange as it may sound, there is such a thing as an "unforgiven" Christian. This is not a statement about ultimate destinies. To be unforgiven in this sense means that the channel of God's grace is blocked from the human side. In particular, it means that you have chosen to hang on to your bitterness and to forfeit your daily walk with the Lord. You would rather be angry than joyful. You have chosen resentment over peace. Your grudges have become more important to you than the daily blessing of God. You would rather live with the "hidden torturers" than experience the freedom of forgiveness.

If you are a Christian—a genuine believer in Jesus Christ—unless you forgive, you will not be forgiven.[5] Why? Because God has already forgiven your sins 100 percent by the blood of Jesus Christ. How dare you, then, be unforgiving to someone who hurt you? That's really the issue. How dare you be unforgiving after what Jesus Christ did for you on the cross?

THE REAL CONDITION OF FORGIVENESS

The real condition of the forgiveness of sins is a repentant heart. Would we not all agree on that? Before you can be forgiven, there must be true repentance before God. And what is the mark of a penitent heart if it is not a forgiving spirit toward other people? As John Stott puts it, "God forgives only the penitent and one of the chief evidences of true penitence is a forgiving spirit."[6] How can you even talk about wanting your sins forgiven if you're holding grudges against other people? You're asking God to do for you what you are unwilling to do for others.

Our real problem at this point is not theological. Our real problem is personal. *We don't see ourselves as great sinners; therefore, we do not appreciate how greatly God has forgiven us.* But when your own sins seem small, the sins of others against you will seem big indeed. The reverse is also true. The greater you see the depth of your sin before God, the less the sins of other people against you will bother you.

If you think you're not much of a sinner, then the offenses of other people are going to appear in your eyes as big. To paraphrase Matthew Henry, "He who relents is he who repents." Don't talk about repentance unless you are willing to forgive your brothers and sisters. Unless you are willing to forgive, your repentance is just so much hot air and empty talk. True repentance always starts with a change of mind that leads to a change of heart that leads to a change (in this case) in the way we view those who have sinned against us.[7]

NEEDED: A SERIOUS MORAL INVENTORY

Jesus is telling us that there is a vital link between the way you treat other people and the way God in heaven is going to treat you. Let's face it. We don't like that. We'd much prefer if we could just have our relationship with God insulated and encapsulated so we could treat other people any way we like. Jesus says, "No deal. You can't have it that way." Unless you forgive, you will not be forgiven. This is a hard word, isn't it? But it is a hard word of grace. Many of us desperately need to take a searching moral inventory and ask ourselves some serious questions:

- Am I up-to-date on my forgiving?
- Am I holding a grudge against anyone?
- Do I harbor bitterness against any person?
- Have I forgiven those closest to me who have hurt me so deeply?

Someone says, "But I can't forgive." No, don't ever say that. The word *can't* is a cop-out. The issue is deeper than that. You won't forgive. Don't make excuses, and don't play games. If you are a true Christian, a genuine believer in Jesus Christ—if your sins have been washed away—then you can forgive. What God has done for you, you can do for others. There may be some people who *won't* forgive. *As long as you won't forgive, you're better off if you never pray the Lord's Prayer because unless you forgive, you will not be forgiven.*

And in all of this we have the example of our Lord Jesus Christ who, when he was crucified—the innocent for the guilty, the just for the unjust, the righteous for the unrighteous—Jesus, who was murdered at the hands of wicked men, as he hung on the cross cried out, "Father, forgive them; for they know not what they do" (Luke 23:34 KJV).

A PLACE TO BEGIN

Let's wrap up this chapter with three simple statements of application.

1. You are never closer to the grace of Jesus Christ than when you confess your sins to him. Are you laboring under a burden of guilt because of foolish things you have said or done? A sense of your own sin is a sign of God's grace at work in your heart. When you cry out, "God be merciful to me, a sinner," you will find that the Father will not turn you away.

2. You are never more like Jesus than when you forgive those who have sinned against you. Do you want to be like Jesus?

Become a great forgiver. Jesus was a forgiving man. He came to create a race of forgiving men and women.

3. You will never fully enter into your freedom in Christ until you learn the freedom of forgiveness. The two freedoms go together. As long as you hold on to your resentments, you are still chained to the past. You only hurt yourself. By refusing to forgive, you block off the channel of God's blessing in your life. Although there is freedom in Christ, the unforgiving Christian knows nothing about it. He is still in bondage to the remembered hurts from the past. Until those chains are broken by a decisive act of forgiveness, he will remain a slave to the past.

I have said several times that this is a hard word, and indeed it is. But it is also a cleaning word that cuts through all our flimsy excuses and leads us to a fountain of grace where we can be healed, made whole, and restored to a right relationship with our Creator. Our God freely forgave us while we were his enemies. Can we not do for others what he has done for us?

The word of the Lord remains. Unless you forgive, you will not be forgiven.

GOING DEEPER

1. What are some of the "debts" for which you need forgiveness by God? How is the blood of Christ the ground of our forgiveness?

2. Why did Jesus single out this petition for further commentary in Matthew 6:14–15?

PRAYER

Father in heaven,

We thank you for the cleansing Word of God that cuts through all of our flimsy excuses.

We praise you because that same Word of God is also able to make us whole and right in your eyes.

O God, may we not fight against your work in us.

Help us to become great forgivers that we ourselves might be forgiven, cleansed, and strengthened to walk closely with you this week.

We ask it in the name of Jesus who made our forgiveness possible.

Amen.

3. Which comes first—God's forgiving us or our forgiving others? Why is the order crucial in properly understanding this petition and the parable of Matthew 18:21–35?

4. Do you agree that even though we are justified by grace, Christians still need to pray for daily forgiveness from the Lord?

5. Name some of the "hidden torturers" that torment us when we refuse to forgive others? How have you experienced this in your own life?

6. Why is it often hard for us to forgive those who have sinned against us? How does our own pride play into our refusal to forgive? Why is humility necessary on our part to forgive others?

AN ACTION STEP

Perhaps you need to make a trip to the cemetery of forgiveness. To do that you need to take your Bible, a pen, and a piece of paper, and find a quiet place. Ask the Lord to bring to your mind the sins of others against you. Write down whatever comes to mind. Then write at the top of the list the word *FORGIVEN*. Then dispose of the list by burning it, burying it, flushing it, or ripping it into tiny pieces. As you do, recall the words of Psalm 103:12, "As far as the east is from the west, so far has he removed our transgressions from us." Ask God to give you his forgiving grace to do the same toward those who have sinned against you.

A TRUTH TO REMEMBER:

True repentance always starts with a change of mind that leads to a change in the way we view those who have sinned against us.

"And lead us not into temptation."
MATTHEW 6:13

CHAPTER EIGHT

DOES GOD LEAD HIS CHILDREN INTO TEMPTATION?

Before we begin: What is the difference between temptation and testing? How can a temptation to sin become an avenue for spiritual growth?

DOES GOD LEAD HIS CHILDREN INTO temptation? This is not an easy question to answer. We know what the word *lead* means, or at least we think we do. And we know what *temptation* means, or at least we know what it is when we yield to it. If we are to pray, "Lead us not into temptation," does that mean God might lead us into temptation under some circumstances? If so, what kind of temptation? And why would

God deliberately lead his children into something he warns them to avoid?

As I sometimes do when I'm unable to answer a heavy question like this, I convened my own theological committee to help me discuss the matter. The committee met during a family trip to Benton Harbor, Michigan. After we finished picking peaches (a basket for about $7.50), we got in the minivan and headed back to Chicago. At that point I convened the committee and raised the question posed by the title of this chapter.

"Do you think," I asked, "that God would ever lead his children into temptation?"

My middle son, Mark, who is our resident theologian, answered immediately. "No, because God is trying to keep us away from temptation."

That's an astute observation. So the answer is no, God does not lead us into temptation.

Then I asked my mother-in-law, who was traveling with us. "Mom, do you think that God leads us into temptation?"

She thought for a minute and then replied, "Maybe. I'm not sure. Sometimes I think he does, and sometimes I think that he doesn't." So the answer is no, and then it's maybe.

So I asked my wife for her opinion: "Do you think that God leads his children into temptation?"

She answered without hesitation, "Yes, of course he does. He leads us into temptations, testings, and trials in order to make us stronger."

Well, there you have it. The answer is no, maybe, and yes.

In order to break the tie, I asked my oldest son the same question: "Joshua, do you think that God leads his children into temptation?"

His answer was, "I asked you first." That wasn't true, of course. He was just stalling for time. And he eventually came in on his mother's side—always a safe thing for a son to do. He said, "Yes," but would give no reason.

We asked our youngest son Nick, and he chimed in on the side of Mark, "No, God does not lead us into temptation."

WALKING AND TALKING

Thus fortified with the answer to my question, I pondered the answer myself. We got home, and a couple of hours later I took a long walk. I usually walk down Greenfield across Oak Park and Harlem and Lathrop and down to Park Avenue in River Forest and back again. It's about four miles. Normally I walk alone. I was walking down Greenfield when a car came by. I took a look at it, and I thought I recognized the person and waved. The car went on and then stopped. It turned out to be a friend from church. Gary came up to me, and we began to talk. "Why don't we walk together?" he said.

Gary walked with me about a mile and a half down Greenfield and then back again. And while we were walking, we discussed the question, Does God lead his children into temptation? Our eventual conclusion was that we didn't know the answer to the question. We parted company on Monday, not having solved the problem. It just happened that I was already scheduled to have lunch with him on Friday of that same week.

When we sat down in the restaurant, his first words to me were, "Pastor, have you figured out the answer to the question yet?" I said, "Sure. It's yes, no, and maybe." He smiled and shook his head.

It is a good question. Does God lead his children into temptation? It is possible to answer yes, or no, or maybe, depending on how you define your terms. As I studied the matter further, I discovered that the early church was concerned about this issue. Because the first Christians held the Lord's Prayer in high esteem, they debated the meaning of this petition over and over. A quick survey of the commentaries reveals that there is a tremendous amount of disagreement about this question, or at least many different answers are given to the question, Does God lead his children into temptation? At one point I had thirty-five different books on my desk all opened trying to find the answers to that question. I didn't find thirty-five different answers, but I found more than two or three.

A PRAYER FOR SPIRITUAL PROTECTION

On one level this petition appears to be simple. Seen from one angle, it appears to mean something like, "Lord, keep us from trouble. Don't let anything really bad happen to us." As a matter of fact, all the commentators agree that this petition is essentially a request to God for spiritual protection. But that still does not answer the central question the text raises: Does God lead his children into temptation?

Let me give you my answer. It all depends on how you define the word *temptation*. The Greek word for *temptation* has two basic meanings. By itself it is a neutral term. It can mean something positive, or it can mean something negative. In its positive meaning it can be, and often is, translated by such words as *trial* or *testing.* In those cases it refers to a difficult circumstance in your life brought about by God in order to improve the quality of your faith and trust in him. In its negative meaning it refers to temptation in the usual English sense of the word—to seduce or lure or solicit to do evil. So this one Greek word can have two different meanings. It can mean a difficult trial, or it can mean a solicitation to do evil.

Your answer to the question, Does God lead his children into temptation? is going to be radically affected by the meaning you think is dominant in Matthew 6. To make matters just a bit more complicated, this word was sometimes used with both meanings present in the same passage of Scripture. For instance, James 1:2 says, "Consider it a great joy, my brothers, whenever you experience various trials" (HCSB). The Greek word for *trials* is the same word used in Matthew 6. The meaning is something like this: "Rejoice when you face trials and hardships and difficulties of many kinds, because you know that the testing of your faith develops perseverance, and perseverance must finish its work so that you may be mature and complete, not lacking in anything." In this sense the word is positive. *James is telling us that God uses trials and difficulties to produce spiritual maturity in your life.*

Now drop down to verse 13 of the same chapter: "No one undergoing a trial should say, 'I am being tempted by God.' For God is not tempted by evil, and He Himself does not tempt anyone" (HCSB). Here the word translated *tempt* or *tempted,* or *tempting* is the verb form of the same word used in James 1:2. The same word is used in a positive sense in verse 2 and a negative sense in verse 13. Here we have one Greek word with two different meanings used without any contradiction at all by the same biblical writer in the same passage. He assumed his readers would be able to understand the difference.

One point is crucial to understanding: *God does not solicit his children to do evil.* God will not lure you into evil. He will not seduce you into evil. In that sense God will never tempt you to do that which is wrong. James 1:13 says that clearly. God will not deliberately bring you into evil. He will never lead you to a place where you are forced to do evil. You may find yourself in a tough spot, and under pressure you may choose to do evil. In your mind you feel forced by the circumstances to do wrong, but even in those cases the choice is yours, not God's. Said another way, God never sets us up to fail. To do that would contradict both his holiness and his love. *So if the question is, Does God lead his children into temptation—in the sense of directly and personally seducing them to do wrong—the answer to that question must always be no.*

CRUCIAL QUESTIONS

I've already said that the Greek word also contains the idea of trials or testings. I think this is probably the primary meaning of the word in Matthew 6:13. Please notice I said the primary meaning—perhaps not the exclusive meaning. I think it probably means trials and testings. The negative meaning may also be present to some degree. But to say that raises a couple of questions. *If it means solicitation to do evil and if we know that God does not solicit us to do evil, when we pray, "Lead us not into temptation," are we asking God not to do that which he said he would never do?* That would seem to be rather nonsensical. *If we know that trials and testings are good for us, and if they are necessary for our spiritual growth, and we should rejoice in them, and if they build us up in the faith, then when we pray, "Lead us not into trials and testings," are we asking God to exempt us from that which is necessary for our own spiritual maturity?* How can we ask God to lead us away from that which is ultimately in our own best interest?

What's the answer to this conundrum? What's the solution to this curious petition of the Lord's Prayer? The key is the double meaning of the Greek word translated *temptation.* These meanings—which seem to be entirely opposite to us—are perhaps not really so far apart, which is why the biblical writers could use the word in both senses in the same passage. That fact gives us a clue to the interpretation of this passage of Scripture.

TESTED BY GOD, TEMPTED BY SATAN

Here is a key statement for understanding this part of the Lord's Prayer. What God gives to us as a trial or a test is almost always used by Satan as a temptation. The same event may be both a trial and test to you and also a temptation from Satan. Or if you will, God uses it to accomplish one thing in your life, and Satan at the same time is working through that event to try to accomplish something diametrically opposite. Often God allows a trial to come for a positive purpose, but Satan tries to co-opt it for his own evil reasons.

The temptation of Jesus in the wilderness offers a clear example of this principle. We know that the devil came to Jesus in the wilderness on three different occasions, tempting him to turn away from the path of obedience to his Heavenly Father. Matthew 4:1 tells us that "Jesus was led up by the Spirit into the desert to be tempted by the Devil." Who did the leading? The Holy Spirit. Who did the tempting? The devil. Is there a contradiction here? Not at all. Did God know what was going to happen when he sent his Son into the desert? Yes, he did. He intended from the beginning to demonstrate that his Son would not yield to Satan's blandishments. Was God tempting his own Son? No, he wasn't. Was God putting his son in a place where his Son could be tempted by the devil? The answer to that must be yes.

That is an amazing thought. At this point we need to think carefully and clearly. I do not believe that God ever directly solicits his children to sin. I don't believe that because the Bible specifically denies it. *But it is also true that from time to time God allows his children to go into a place where they will face severe temptations from Satan.* Is God responsible for the severe temptation? No, he's not. He does the leading; Satan does the tempting. From God's point of view it's a test. From Satan's point of view it's a temptation.

We see this pattern occurring in every area of life. *God sends a trial, and Satan turns it into a temptation.* Let's suppose a child of God contracts a deadly sickness. Could that sickness be a testing from God? Yes, it could. It almost always is a testing from God to purify motives, to cause the child of God to look away from the things of earth to the things of heaven, and to turn the eyes of the child of God back to the Lord. Many good things are accomplished through sickness in the life of the believer. Does Satan work through sickness? Yes, he does. And through that same sickness Satan will be working to tempt you to despair, to anger, to bitterness, and ultimately to turn away from the Lord. What God intends for your spiritual good is the avenue Satan uses to pull you down.

Or suppose you lose your job. You say, "Could that be from God?" Yes, it could. If you lose your job, could God have a better purpose in mind for you? Yes, and he often does. He may have a better job for you. He certainly wants to build some spiritual character in your life. You may have fallen in love with the things of the world to the point where those good things have become an idol to you. In that case it is good for you to lose a good job. And during that trial from God, Satan will tempt you to anger, despair, and discouragement.

It works the other way, too. Let's suppose you get a promotion and a nice raise in salary. Now you are better off financially than you've ever been. Can a promotion be a trial from God? Absolutely. Prosperity is often a trial or testing from God to see how you will handle his blessings. Prosperity ought to make us more generous toward the needy. Having more ought to open our eyes to those who have less than we do. But that same prosperity often makes us greedy, selfish, and blind to the less fortunate.

Let's take the case of a businessman on the seventh day of a long trip. He checks into his motel room, tired and lonely. On top of the television is one of those boxes where they bring in those movies rated X or XX or XXX. The man knows that he has no business pushing that button. But when he's alone and spiritually disoriented, he feels a strong urge to watch one of those movies. Does God know the box is there? Yes, he does. Did God allow his servant to go into that room? Yes, he did. Is it a test? Yes, it is. And if the man passes the test, he will be stronger spiritually because he said no. Is it a temptation? Yes, it is. It's a temptation to reach over and touch that box and give in to lust.

TWO CONCLUSIONS

Those are just a few examples of how something God intends as a means of building you up is also used by Satan as a means of temptation to pull you down. I draw two conclusions. *First, testings and trials are a normal part of the Christian life.* They are part of God's curriculum for you. He puts difficult choices in front of you every day so that by following him and by trusting him in those circumstances you become stronger. Your faith becomes confirmed, and you become an example to other people of victory over the world, the flesh, and the devil. There's nothing you can do to escape the trials of life—nothing at all. In the school of grace, God doesn't offer a "no trials" degree program. All of us will be tested many times in many ways.[1]

Second, a trial becomes a temptation when we respond wrongly. That which was sent into our life in order to make us stronger actually tears us down and makes us weaker when we respond in the power of the flesh. What God means for good, Satan means for evil. The Christian hangs in the balance between the tests and the trials from the Heavenly Father and the perversions of Satan as he twists that which God gives us and whispers in our ear, "Go ahead. Go ahead. Go ahead."

Could this be the reason the biblical writers did not sharply distinguish what we want to keep separate? We separate trials and temptations as if they are far, far apart. The biblical writers had no problem using the same word to mean trials in one verse and then using the same word to mean temptations just a few verses later. They understood what we have forgotten. Everything good comes from God, and everything he gives us is ultimately for our good and his glory. He does not sin, nor does he solicit us to sin. But hidden inside every trial is the seed of a temptation that Satan uses to harvest a crop of evil in our lives.

William Barclay points out that this petition is the most natural and instinctive part of the Lord's Prayer.[2] Since all of us are put to the test in one way or another all the time, we all understand what it means to pray for deliverance, for "help in the time of need." Hebrews 4:15 points us to the Lord Jesus as the one who can help us when we cry out to him because he was "tempted in every way, just as we are—yet was without sin." The King James Version tells us that he was "touched with the feeling of our infirmities." Jesus is "touched" by the weakness of our feeble flesh. *Whatever touches us touches him.* To say "I feel your pain" has become a cliché today, but in Jesus' case it is true. He is moved by our sorrow, aware of our tears, and touched by our failure. He knows what we are going through.

Sometimes when we are in the middle of a hard time, people who mean well will say to us, "I know what you are going through." That is often a cruel thing to say. How can you be sure you know what another person is thinking or feeling? It is better never to say that because if you really do know what another person is going through, your heart will make that clear to them. And if you don't, it's better not to say anything at all. As I pondered this truth, an incident came to mind that I haven't thought about in a long time. The story starts with a good friend from my growing-up years in a small Alabama town. We used to wrestle in his front yard, and then we would go inside his house and watch television. In my mind's eye I can still see the room where we played games and read comic books by the hour. When we were in the seventh grade, our class went on a trip up the Natchez Trace with our youth group. Evidently he got some kind of infection or virus. The next day he died suddenly. It was the first time I had ever been that close to death. I remember going to his funeral and being too frightened to walk by the casket.

Now fast-forward the story almost ten years when my father died after a brief illness. Because he was a beloved physician, everyone in town came to pay their respects. People I didn't know told me stories about my father. Men and women wept openly at the funeral home. After all these years the events surrounding my father's death are a blur in my memory. I recall hundreds of people stopping by to express their sympathy, but I don't remember what anyone said. Except for one person. The scene is etched clearly in my mind although it could not have lasted more than twenty seconds.

I was sitting in a bedroom at home talking with some friends. In came the father of my friend who had died a decade earlier.

He put his arm on my shoulder and said, "Ray, we're so sorry to hear about your father. He was a good man. If there is anything we can do, let us know." That was it. A few words and he was gone. But what a message those few words conveyed. Because I knew that he knew what it meant to lose someone you love, his words are the only ones that have stayed with me since my father's death more than a quarter-century ago.

That's what Hebrews 4:15 means when it says that Jesus is touched with the feeling of our infirmities. He knows our pain; he sees our weakness; he understands what we are going through. Because he was a "man of sorrows and acquainted with grief," he truly knows what we are experiencing.

C. S. LEWIS ON TEMPTATION

And how good it is to know that he was tempted just as we are. *Jesus faced every kind of temptation we can face.* Basically every temptation falls into one of three categories: the lust of the eyes, the lust of the flesh, and the pride of life (cf. 1 John 2:14–17). Jesus defeated the devil in those three areas. Where we fail, he succeeded. Where we give in, he stood strong. Where we collapse under pressure, Jesus obeyed his Father. He was tempted, yet he never sinned by giving in. I find great comfort in these words of C. S. Lewis in his book *Mere Christianity:*

> A silly idea is current that good people do not know what temptation means. This is an obvious lie. Only those who try to resist temptation know how strong it is. After all, you find out the strength of the German army by fighting against it, not by giving in. You find out the

> strength of a wind by trying to walk against it, not by lying down. A man who gives in to temptation after five minutes simply does not know what it would have been like an hour later. That is why bad people, in one sense, know very little about badness. They have lived a sheltered life by always giving in. . . . Christ, because he was the only man who never yielded to temptation, is also the only man who knows to the full what temptation means.[3]

This has enormous implications for our spiritual life. Because Christ was tempted and never gave in, we may be sure that he is never surprised by anything we say or do. We give in too early, so we never feel the full force of temptation. But Jesus let the waves of temptation rush over him and stood like the Rock of Gibraltar. When we pray, we don't have to worry that we will somehow shock him. He's heard it all and seen it all. We can go ahead and be totally honest about our failures. He knows about it even before we tell him.

RON DUNN AND JESUS

And we don't have to prove ourselves worthy when we pray. Ron Dunn learned this lesson at the end of a very bad day. When he got up, he didn't spend time praying. As the day wore on, he was churlish in the way he treated people. When the day finally ended, he knelt to pray and began by saying, "Lord, I've made a mess of my life today, and I confess I'm not worthy to come into your presence."

At that point he felt the Lord interrupt his prayer. "Ron, do you think having a quiet time this morning would have made you worthy to talk to me? Do you think doing good and treating people right would have somehow made you qualified to come into the presence of God? If that's what you think, you don't know yourself, you don't know me, and you don't understand the grace of God." I can relate to that story because most of the time that's exactly how I think. It's so easy for all of us to believe that our good works somehow commend us to God, that if we'll just "be good," God is more likely to hear our prayers.[4]

To think like that is to deny the gospel itself. We are accepted by God only on the basis of what Jesus Christ has done. How dare we wave the tattered rags of a quiet time and think that somehow that makes a difference in heaven. I'm all for having a quiet time and for treating people right and totally on the side of living for the Lord, but all of that cannot add even a tiny sliver to our acceptance before God. It is either all by grace or not by grace at all. Because Jesus knows how sinful we really are, we don't have to play games when we pray. We can come to God just the way we are, clinging only to the cross and claiming nothing but the blood of Jesus as our own hope of being accepted when we pray.

Not long ago a noted pastor came through Chicago to speak at a pastor's conference. One of his messages dealt with the need to depend wholly on the Lord and not on our own resources. As he came to the close, he told the story of how King Jehoshaphat prayed in 2 Chronicles 20.

The Ammonites and the Moabites were moving in a vast army toward Jerusalem. There were so many of them, and they were so well armed that the men of Israel would never be able to defeat them. As the invaders came closer and closer, the situation looked increasingly hopeless. The king called for a nationwide fast. Men from every town and village gathered in Jerusalem to seek the Lord. Jehoshaphat stood before them and offered one of the greatest prayers in the Bible (2 Chron. 20:6–12). He began by declaring God's greatness: "O LORD, God of our fathers, are you not the God who is in heaven? You rule over all the kingdoms of the nations. Power and might are in your hand, and no one can withstand you" (v. 6). Then he reminded God of the promises he made to take care of his people when they were in trouble. Then he told God, "We're in big trouble now!" He freely admitted, "We have no power to face this vast army that is attacking us" (v. 12). And he concluded with this simple confession: "We do not know what to do, but our eyes are upon you" (v. 12).

God's answer came through a prophet, who told the people to "stand still and see the salvation of the Lord." The next day Jehoshaphat put the male singers at the head of the army and sent them out to do battle. They literally stood still and watched as the Lord sent confusion into the enemy ranks. The Moabites and Ammonites started killing each other by mistake. The great slaughter was followed by the plundering of the supplies left behind by the enemy soldiers. The story ends with the army of the Lord gathering for a praise celebration, giving thanks to God for the victory he provided.

After telling that story, the pastor commented that when Jehoshaphat prayed, "We do not know what to do, but our eyes are upon you," he was really saying, "Lord, we're just a bunch of pathetic losers. And if you don't help us, we're sunk." He went on to say that he had discovered that this was the true mission statement of the church he pastors: "We're just a bunch of pathetic losers, and if God doesn't help us, we're sunk." That's a good name for a church: The Church of the Pathetic Losers. A church like that would never run out of prospects.

BLUNDER FORWARD

I think he's absolutely right. Apart from God's grace, that's all we are—just a bunch of pathetic losers. *Without God we don't have a chance, we don't have a thing to offer, and we don't even know what to do next.* Sometimes I think the hardest job God has is getting his children to admit how desperately they need him. A friend told me about a pastor at another church in the Chicago area who preached something similar. He came up with a phrase that he printed at the top of their church bulletins, even though some of the leaders didn't feel comfortable with it: "Blunder Forward." Having been a pastor for nearly a quarter of a century, I can testify how true that is. Even on our best days, we struggle as God's people simply to "blunder forward." And some days we can't even do that.

The fifth petition of the Lord's Prayer is meant for pathetic losers. But that should not discourage us in the least. God does his best work with pathetic losers who will cast themselves wholly on his grace. Jesus told us how to live when he declared,

PRAYER

Loving Lord,

We truly believe that all things work together for good to those who love you.

When we are tempted to sin, give us wisdom to choose the way of escape while we have the chance.

May we not trifle with sin and so be brought down in shame and disgrace.

Give us a strong desire to do the right thing no matter what it costs.

Help us to see your fingerprints even in the hard experiences of life.

May our trials make us more like Jesus day by day.

Amen.

"For whoever wants to save his life will lose it, but whoever loses his life because of Me and the gospel will save it" (Mark 8:35 HCSB). In the kingdom of God, all the values of the world are reversed. The way up is down. The last shall be first. The least will be the greatest. The servants will be the leaders.

When we pray, "Lead us not into temptation," we are admitting that we have no power and no clue how to face the problems of life. God delights to help those who have nowhere else to go but to the Lord.

Satan wants something from us in the moment of temptation, and so does God!

GOING DEEPER

1. Why is it important to remember that God never solicits us to do evil? What happens when we forget this truth?

2. What are the biggest temptations you face on a daily basis?

3. Can you think of a time when a trial became a temptation to sin because you responded wrongly? What did you learn from that experience?

4. Consider the C. S. Lewis quote in this chapter. What encouragement do you take from the fact that though Christ was severely tempted, he never sinned?

A TRUTH TO REMEMBER:

Satan wants something from us in the moment of temptation, and so does God!

5. Do you agree that apart from the grace of God we are "pathetic losers"? How do we square that truth with the reality

that in Christ we have been blessed with every spiritual blessing in the heavenly places (Eph. 1:3)? Is there a contradiction here? In what sense are both perspectives important in maintaining a proper spiritual balance?

6. Read the story of Joseph and Potiphar's wife in Genesis 39. How did the temptation arise, and how did Joseph respond? How was this incident both a temptation to evil and a testing from the Lord?

AN ACTION STEP

Memorize 1 Corinthians 10:13 this week. Ask God for spiritual sensitivity so that you will quickly take the "way of escape" when you are tempted to sin.

"But deliver us from the evil one."
MATTHEW 6:13

CHAPTER NINE
DELIVER US FROM EVIL

Before we begin: If you were Satan, how would you attack the children of God? How can our failures prepare us for greater things in the future?

NOT LONG AGO I GOT AN E-MAIL from my college roommate—a man I haven't seen since the day we graduated together. He wrote to ask if I had heard the news. What news? Another friend from our college days had divorced his wife and was now pursuing the former wife of a classmate from those same college days. Two friends, two marriages broken, one man now pursuing his former friend's former wife. To make matters worse, the man doing the pursuing was a pastor.

Then just a few days later I received another E-mail, this time from a friend I met during my seminary days. I haven't seen him since we graduated. He wrote me a nice note that included these two sentences: "In this world of ours it is never a sure thing, never to be assumed that a seminary grad or pastor is continuing in the faith. I have heard too many horror stories of broken marriages and wrecked ministries."

Those two messages set me to thinking. I was struck by the fact that I received them so close in time from friends who don't know each other and whom I haven't seen in over twenty years. Yet they said nearly identical things. I do not bring up those examples simply to bemoan the fact that spiritual leaders fall into grievous sin; that much is evident from a simple reading of the Bible. There is Noah who got drunk, Abraham who lied about his wife, Moses who murdered an Egyptian, and of course there is David who committed adultery and then had a man murdered to cover up his sin.

BUT FOR THE GRACE OF GOD

Why does God allow such things to happen? I'm sure we all know one answer already. *God allows Christian leaders to fall into sin so that the rest of us will learn not to make the same stupid mistake.* That's true, of course. How many of us have heard bad news about a friend and said, "There but for the grace of God go I"? I have said that to myself many times, and so have you. It's perfectly true that we can all take a lesson from the mistakes of others, and if we don't, we may find ourselves wishing we had. As John Newton put it in his hymn "Amazing Grace," there are many "dangers, toils, and snares" on the road from earth to heaven. It is only the grace of God that keeps any of us safe along the way.

That brings us to the second half of the fifth petition of the Lord's Prayer: "Lead us not into temptation, but deliver us from the evil one." The word *deliver* is strong. It means to rescue or to snatch. To deliver from what? Either from "evil" or "the evil one." The KJV has "evil," and the NIV and most other modern translations have "the evil one." Which is correct? Are we to pray to be delivered from evil in general, or are we to pray for specific deliverance from Satan and his power? In one sense there is not a huge difference between those two.

John Calvin suggested that the interpretation is not hugely affected either way. But something can be said for using the phrase "the evil one." When this particular Greek verb is used with this particular preposition, it almost always means to rescue from a specific person, not from an abstract idea like evil. And as we have already seen, in Matthew 4, Jesus was personally tempted by the devil himself. In this context, then, I think our Lord Jesus is warning his disciples not of evil in general but of the archenemy of the believer—of Satan himself, of the devil and his power. Therefore, we can understand this petition this way: "Lead us not into temptation, but deliver us, snatch us, save us, from Satan and his evil schemes against us."

Next to this petition you should write down 1 Peter 5:8, "Be sober! Be on the alert! Your adversary the Devil is prowling around like a roaring lion, looking for anyone he can devour" (HCSB). Be self-controlled and alert. Your enemy the devil prowls around like a roaring lion looking for someone to devour." Seen in that light, the second half of this petition is easy to understand. "O God, don't let Satan loose on me. O God, rescue me from Satan and his marauding power and his destructive force in my life." It's a personal prayer. "O God, when Satan comes near me, protect me from his power." *This petition is really a confession of our spiritual weakness.* It's a prayer of those who feel their vulnerability in the face of Satan and all his attacks. When we pray this prayer, we are saying, "O Heavenly Father, don't let me come to the place where I will succumb to temptation. Don't let me come to the place where I will be overwhelmed by Satan, but deliver me from Satan and his power in my life."

When you pray, "Lead us not into temptation," you are expressing your own weakness in the face of the trials and difficulties of life. You are saying, "Lord, by myself I cannot make it. By myself I can't do it." When you pray, "But deliver us from the evil one," you declare your confidence in God's mighty power. *The first half is your weakness. The second half is God's power.*

WAS JESUS A COWARD?

To say it like that is to raise a crucial question. Is this a prayer for cowards? Is this a prayer for people who are too frightened to do spiritual warfare? Let me answer that by asking a question in return. Was Jesus a coward? The answer of course is no. But Matthew 26 says that in the Garden of Gethsemane, on the night before he was crucified, the Son of God knelt and begged God for the cup to pass from him. The Bible says he prayed with loud cries and tears to God to be delivered from that which was before him. He was the Son of God. Yet in the moment of his trial, he did not boast of his power. He didn't say, "O God, I'm ready to go. O God, I'm strong. I'll crawl up on that cross and die." On the night before it happened, he cried out to God for help.

The victory of Calvary was won on Thursday night. The battle was won before Judas ever planted his betrayer's kiss. The battle was won before a spike was ever nailed in the hands of Jesus. The battle was won when he prayed. *He did not fail in his testing because he did not fail in his praying.* That thought deserves our careful concentration. Our Lord Jesus did not fail in his testing because he did not fail in his praying. The conclusion is obvious. If our Lord needed to pray, how much more do we need to cry out in the face of the things that are before us?

Jot down Luke 22:40 next to Matthew 6:13. Jesus is praying in the Garden of Gethsemane. We pick up the story in verse 39. "Jesus went out . . . and his disciples followed him. On reaching the place, he said to them, 'Pray that you will not fall into temptation.'" Then he went off and prayed earnestly to God and came back and found them asleep. Verse 46 says, "'Why are you sleeping?' he asked them. 'Get up and pray so that you will not fall into temptation.'"

These verses explain Matthew 6:13. In the moment of crisis, Jesus passed the test because he did not fail to pray. Jesus' word to his disciples and his word to us is simple: Before you face what the world has to offer and before you go to do battle with Satan, make sure you have prayed. Pray that you may not fall into temptation. In the words of one writer, "The battle is half-won if you want to avoid temptation enough to beg God to help you." When you pray, you are admitting your weakness. When you don't pray, it's usually because you don't take temptation seriously.

A LITTLE FEAR IS A HEALTHY THING

This petition is a warning against being cocksure. It's a warning against taking our own strength for granted. When the soldier goes out to do battle, is it not better if he is a little bit afraid? Is it not true that a little fear can keep a soldier alive on the battlefield? The presumptuous soldier who rushes off to battle is the one most likely to be killed in combat. Suppose we flip this petition over and view it from the other side. Suppose someone were to pray, "Go ahead, Lord. Let me have it. I can handle temptation. I'm strong. I'm ready. I can take whatever Satan throws at me." Such a person is headed for a rude awakening. He is defeated before he steps on the battlefield because he has taken the adversary too lightly.

A little fear is healthy. Jesus is saying, "You're too weak to face the devil on your own, so don't even try. You're weak, but God is strong. You in your own strength are no match for Satan." Yet when you are in the motel room by yourself, if you are trusting in your own strength, you'll go over and push that button, and then you'll curse yourself afterwards for having done it. You'll be defeated every time. *A little fear is a healthy motivation when you're fighting against a superhuman adversary.*

This petition, which on the surface seems simple, is actually profound. It's a prescription for the spiritual life. It's a measure of your spiritual health. Do you pray this prayer? Jesus said, "When you pray, say, lead me not into temptation"—a confession of your own weakness—"but deliver me from the evil one"—a confession of your profound confidence in God and his power. When you pray this way, you will find that no matter what happens to you, you will be delivered. You will not be defeated. You will not fall. God will take you into the temptation. God will take you through it. And no matter how difficult, God will bring you out of it.

This petition forcibly reminds us of how weak we really are. Without the Lord's help, we're in big trouble every moment of every day. We are sitting ducks for the flaming darts of the devil. Unless the Lord helps us, we will not only face temptation, but we will also succumb to it every time.

The words of Jesus to Peter seem to go hand in hand with this petition. At the Last Supper, Jesus predicted that Peter would deny him, and he also predicted that Peter would not be utterly destroyed. He would be tempted, fall, and eventually be restored by the Lord. "Simon, Simon, look out! Satan has asked to sift you like wheat. But I have prayed for you, that your faith may not fail. And you, when you have turned back, strengthen your brothers" (Luke 22:31–32 HCSB).

Twice Jesus calls his name as if to reassure him that even in the midst of his greatest humiliation, the Lord would be with him every step of the way. The words of Christ tie both meanings of *temptation* together. *Satan wants something from us in the moment of temptation, and so does God!* The one would destroy us, and the other wants to deliver us. In this case Satan's temporary victory in Peter's life leads to a much greater victory for God in the end. So it is for us as well. Our defeats, bitter as they are, can lead to great spiritual victories.

SATAN'S DESIRE

"Simon, Simon, look out! Satan has asked to sift you like wheat" (Luke 22:31 HCSB). The word translated "has asked" is a bit stronger in the Greek. It means something like a strong demand. Satan set his eyes on Peter and determined to bring him down by any means possible. *I find it comforting that Satan must ask God's permission before touching any of his children.*

Sometimes Christians become frozen in fear because they have given Satan too much credit. Sometimes we talk as if Satan were a kind of "Junior God," almost God but not quite, as if he has 90 percent of God's power, 90 percent of his wisdom, and so on. But that is quite different from the biblical picture. Satan is always revealed as a creature of great power and cunning who is nevertheless first and always a created being. He has no power independent of God. He can do only what God permits him to do. As Martin Luther put it, the devil is "God's devil." One Puritan writer called him "God's lapdog." Surely this is more biblical than viewing him as some evil force equal with God. If he is God's equal, he wouldn't have to ask permission before attacking Peter.

Note also that the "you" in this verse is plural. Satan wanted to destroy all the apostles, but he specifically targeted Peter. This makes sense when you think about it. *Satan goes after spiritual leaders.* He starts at the top because if he can knock off the leader, others will no doubt fall in short order. That's why the devil goes after leaders first—elders, pastors, deacons, teachers, leaders, and parents. His desire is to "sift" God's people by putting them under such pressure that they will give way and their faith will be proved spurious. If that is the case, why would God permit his children to be put in such a bad position? Precisely so that he can prove that even under severe pressure, we can survive if we depend on his grace. In Peter's case that meant actually falling into sin and being restored later.

Satan often attacks us at the point of our perceived strength, not at the point of our weakness. After all, had not Peter boldly said, "Even if everyone falls, yet I will not" (Mark 14:29 HCSB)? If you had asked Peter six hours earlier to name his strong points, no doubt he would have listed boldness and courage right at the top. He would have said, "Sometimes I put my foot in my mouth, but at least I'm not afraid to speak up. Jesus knows that I'll always be there when he needs me." But when Satan attacked, it came so suddenly, so swiftly, so unexpectedly that the bold apostle turned to butter. By himself Peter was helpless. In the moment of crisis, Peter failed at the point where he pledged to be eternally faithful.

Should this surprise us? After all, why should Satan attack only at the point of your self-perceived weakness? *If you know you have a weakness, that's the area you will guard most carefully.* If you know you have a problem with anger or with laziness or with lust or with gluttony, will you not be on your guard lest you fall? But it is not so with your strengths. You tend to take those areas for granted. You say, "That's not a problem for me. I have other problems, but that area is not really a temptation at all."

Watch out! Put up the red flag! There is danger ahead. When a person takes any area of life for granted, that's the one area Satan is most likely to attack. Why? Because that's the one area where you aren't watching for his attack.

It happened to Peter. It will happen to you and to me sooner or later.

CHRIST'S PRAYER

"But I have prayed for you, Simon, that your faith may not fail" (Luke 22:32). These simple words contain amazing reservoirs of truth. *First, they tell us that Christ knew in advance everything that Peter was about to do.* He knew about the denials, the cursing, the repeated lies Peter was about to tell, and he knew about the bitter tears he would shed when he saw Christ taken away in judgment. Even more than that, he knew that one day Peter would become a mighty preacher of the gospel. He saw it all—the pride, the reckless boasting, the shameful denials, the broken heart, the deep repentance, and the new resolve to serve the Lord. He saw it all before any of it had happened. He saw it before Peter knew anything about it.

Second, Christ's response to Peter's fall is to pray for him. Hebrews 7:25 tells us that Christ prays for us in heaven, and it is because of his prayers that we are saved "to the uttermost" (KJV). In a deep sense our salvation depends on the moment-by-moment prayers of Jesus for his people. Not in general or by groups but one by one, he prays for us: "Lord, there's Mike, and I know he is struggling. Help him to stay strong. Sharon needs your help, Father. Julio is about to fall into temptation. Don't let him be utterly destroyed. Megan wants to do right. Help her to have the courage she needs." What an awesome thought—that the Son of God prays for us. Without his prayers we would never make it.

Third, Christ does not pray for Peter to be removed from temptation. Instead, he prays that in the midst of his shame he would not lose his faith altogether. "Father, Satan wants to sift him to destroy him altogether. Please don't let that happen." What a revelation this is of God's purposes for you and me. This explains so much about why we go through hard times. Many times God intends that we should face the truth of our own personal failures so that our trust might be in the Lord alone.

PETER'S CONVERSION

"And when you have turned back, strengthen your brothers" (Luke 22:32). The King James says "when thou art converted." Was Peter a believer? Yes, of course, and he had been a believer from the day he left all to follow Christ. *But in some deep sense he had never been fully converted to God.* His shocking failure would be the means God used to finish the conversion process in his soul.

Note the little word *when.* What a word of grace that is! Christ knew all about Peter's coming fall, but he also saw that Peter would one day return to the Lord and be stronger than ever. Theologians call this the doctrine of the perseverance of the saints. It means that those who have trusted Christ will maintain their faith to the end. Years ago I heard someone rephrase the doctrine this way. He called it the doctrine of the perseverance of God and the preservation of the saints. *Because God perseveres with us, we are preserved safe through our many trials.* Do we persevere? Yes, but only because God first perseveres with us. If he didn't, we never would and never could.

I notice two encouraging facts about the way Jesus treated Peter: (1) He never criticized him, and (2) he never gave up on him. Jesus knew about Peter's denial long before it happened. He knew what Peter would do, he knew how he would react, and he knew the kind of man Peter would be afterward. That's why he said, "When you have turned back." Not if but when! He knew that Peter's heart was good; he knew that after his terrible sin he would return to the Lord. Isn't that wonderful? *Jesus had more faith in Peter than Peter had in Jesus.* He knew that Peter had important work to do—"strengthen your brothers"—but it couldn't happen without his fall and his restoration to the Lord. It had to happen that way, or else Peter would never be fully effective for Christ.

An important principle is at work here. A bone that is broken often becomes stronger after it is healed. Something in the healing process actually makes the break point stronger than it was before. The same is true of a rope that breaks. In the hands of a master splicer, the rope once repaired becomes stronger than it was before. The same is true of our failures. *God can touch our broken places and make us stronger than we were before.* Though we fall and though our faces are covered with the muck and grime of bitter defeat, by God's grace we can rise from the field of defeat to march on to new victory. That's what happened to Peter. His guilt was turned into grace; his shame into sympathy; his failure into faithfulness.

WHY GOD ALLOWS US TO FALL

Never again would Peter brag on himself as he did that night. Never again would he presume to be better than his brothers. Never again would he be so cocky and self-confident. All that was gone forever, part of the price Peter paid for his failure in the moment of crisis. *It is good the Lord allows this to happen to us.* By falling flat on our faces, we are forced to admit that without the Lord we can do nothing but fail. The quicker we learn that—and we never learn it completely—the better off we will be. Failure never seems to be a good thing when it happens, but if failure strips away our cocky self-confidence, then failure is ultimately a gift from God.

Years ago I was at a major turning point in my life. As I agonized over the choice before me, some dear friends came to give me their candid advice. At the time I did not want to hear what they had to say. As I listened, I got angrier and angrier until I lost my temper and said some things that I later came to regret deeply. Anger boiled over within me, and words spewed out like hot lava from a volcano. After it was over, I sat shaking in my chair, frightened at the rage that had been pent up within me. Days passed, and the anger within slowly subsided. It was as though once the top had been blown off, I couldn't get it back on again. My anger flared every time I thought of that confrontation.

A month later while attending a conference in another state, I happened to meet a man who was to become a close personal friend. One night we stayed up late, and I told, in exhaustive detail, the story of my personal explosion. As I told it, I got angry all over.

My friend listened to the whole sordid tale, and then he spoke. "Ray, you are a lucky man. What happened to you was a sign of God's grace." I was baffled by his words. Had he missed the point of my story? But he knew me better than I knew myself. "God has shown you his grace by allowing you to lose your temper like that."

How could losing my temper be an act of God's grace? My friend offered a simple explanation: "For many years you've had the image of a man completely in control of his life. You appear on the outside to be laid-back. People who don't know you well think you don't have a worry in the world. And you've cultivated that image because it makes you popular and easy to like. But the truth is far different. There's a seething cauldron inside you that you've managed to keep a lid on for a long time. But that night, the lid came off. Before that night, if anyone had said, 'Do you have a temper?' you would have laughed and said, 'Not really.' You can't say that anymore."

Then he went on to explain a fundamental truth about the Christian life. "As we grow in Christ, most of us come to the place where we think there are some sins we just won't commit. Maybe we don't say it out loud, but in our hearts we think, *I would never do that.* That's what happened to you and your temper. You covered yours for so long that you thought it had gone away. But it was always there, like a snake coiled in the grass, waiting for the chance to strike." He concluded with these penetrating words. "That night God pulled back the cover and let the world see the depravity within your own heart. From now on, whenever you stand up to speak, you can never say, 'I don't have a temper,' because you do. God let you say those terrible things to your friends so that you could never again pretend to be something that you are not. That's the grace of God at work in your life." I believe every word my friend said was absolutely true. God let me fail in the moment of crisis, and in so doing he showed me a part of myself I had never seen before.

That's what he did for Peter. Never again would Peter stand up and boast about his courage. In the future he would talk about humility instead.

GOING OFF THE CLIFF

I have already noted that Jesus knew about Peter's fall and even predicted it, but he never tried to prevent it. This raises an interesting question. If God knows about our failures even before we fail, why doesn't he stop us? Why does he let us go headlong over the cliff? Here are three possible answers.

1. *To show us the depth of our sin.* As long as we stand on top of the cliff, we can brag about our goodness; but when we are lying at the bottom, bruised and broken, we are forced to admit the truth about ourselves.

2. *To purge us from pride.* I don't think Peter ever forgot that sad night when he denied the Lord. Never again would he boastfully claim to be more courageous than the other apostles. So it

is with all of us. Our failures are like Jacob's limp. They serve as a perpetual reminder and a guard against overwhelming pride.

3. *To prepare us for greater work we must do.* In some way we can't fully understand, Peter *had* to fall so that God could raise him back up again. The falling part was Peter's own doing; the raising up came by the gracious hand of the Lord. But there is no getting up without falling down first. Even so our failures qualify us to minister to others we could never otherwise reach. I have seen divorced people who have experienced God's grace greatly used to help others going through that same heartbreak. The same is true of those once trapped by drug and alcohol addiction, sexual sin, and those who have served time in prison. God uses our worst moments as preparation for work he has appointed for us.

God often uses broken people to accomplish great things. If you doubt this, let's do a roll call of broken saints:

- Noah who got drunk
- Abraham who lied about his wife
- Jacob who was a deceiver
- Moses who murdered an Egyptian
- Rahab who was a harlot
- David who was an adulterer
- Paul who persecuted the church
- Peter who denied Christ

Here is an amazing thought to ponder: *Peter did much more for Jesus Christ after his fall than he did before.* Before his fall he was loud, boisterous, and unreliable; afterward he became a flaming preacher of the gospel. Before, he was a big talker; afterward, he talked only of what Jesus Christ could do for others. He was the same man, but he was different. He was still Peter through and through, but he had been sifted by Satan, and in the sifting the chaff of his life had been blown away.

This is what Peter lost in his failure:

- His vanity
- His pride
- His self-confidence
- His rash impulsiveness
- His unreliability

This is what Peter gained after his restoration:

- Humility
- New confidence in God
- Tested courage
- A new determination to serve Jesus Christ
- A willingness to use his experience to help others

The things he lost he didn't really need; the things he gained couldn't have come any other way. In the same way God redeems our mistakes by removing the things that brought us down and replacing them with the qualities we always wanted but couldn't seem to find.

There is much in this story to encourage us. It was not the real Peter who denied the Lord; it was the real Peter who followed him into the courtyard. It was not the real Peter who cursed and swore; it was the real Peter who said, "You are the Christ, the Son of the living God." *When the Lord looks at you and me, he sees beyond our faults to the loyalty underneath.* He sees our pain, our tears, and our earnest desire to please him. He sees us in our faltering attempts to follow him.

IF WE KNEW THE NAKED TRUTH

A friend dropped by my home for a visit. During our conversation he mentioned a family in our church that was going through a hard time. I commented to my friend that if we knew the naked truth about every person in our congregation, we'd all run away screaming. I for one am glad I don't know the truth about everyone. Let's face it. We're all broken people. Some of us just hide our brokenness better than others. There's a little bit of Peter in all of us, and that's why this story speaks on such a deep level.

What should we learn from these words of Christ?

The value of humility. If Christ's handpicked number one man could deny him, then none of us can claim to be beyond temptation. Peter wasn't a bad man, but he was weak, and he didn't realize how weak he was until it was too late. A little humility is always in order. You're not as hot as you think you are . . . and neither am I.

The need for patience with one another. Sometimes we act surprised when our Christian friends disappoint us. Perhaps we should be surprised when they don't. Certainly we'd all be happier if we lowered our expectations to a level consistent with reality. Even on our best days we will still sin and disappoint ourselves and others. It behooves us all to cut one another a little bit of slack.

The magnificence of God's grace. None of us really understands God's grace. This is the hardest of all Christian doctrines to grasp because it goes against our deeply felt need to prove ourselves worthy. Grace says, "You aren't worthy, but I love you anyway." That's hard to hear, hard to believe, and sometimes hard to extend to other Christians. Meditate on grace. Think about it. Rest in it. Rejoice in it. Talk about it. Share it. Sing it.

One friend said she found hope because like Peter she had made her share of mistakes. I replied that people with a past would find comfort in his story. As true as that is, it's also true that we all have a past and, therefore, we all stand in Peter's shoes—greatly loved, capable of foolish choices, and yet redeemed and redeemable for service in the future. This is only possible by the grace of God. This means that the God who forgives our past and our present intends also to forgive our future as well. What an awesome thought that is. As you read these words, take heart. You may be heading for a fall, and you don't know it yet. But the God who loves you enough to let you fall will himself pick you back up again.

"LORD, HAVE MERCY"

In the moment of severe testing, we need the mercy of God. Mercy is what delivers us from trouble. A few weeks ago a friend at the local high school gave me a tape of a speech Gary Olson made in April 1998. Gary was a former elder of our church and for many years was the head football coach at Oak Park–River Forest High School. He made the speech eight months after his heart surgery in 1997 and a year and a half before his sudden death in November 1999.

On the tape Gary is giving a short talk to a group of Christian coaches about handling life's hard times. He began by mentioning his lung cancer in the early 1980s that led to his coming to Christ. Then in 1989, his wife Dawn was in a terrible accident that nearly took her life. Gary stepped down from coaching for a while so he could help her.

The hardest blows came in 1997. In August of that year he collapsed during football practice and was taken to the hospital, where the doctors discovered he had an enlarged heart. A few days later he had surgery to replace a defective heart valve. At about the same time he faced a crisis in his family. A month or so later his mother suddenly died of a brain hemorrhage. It seemed almost too much to bear.

On the tape he said that he had called his pastor and asked, "How should I pray?" His pastor told him to pray, "Lord, have mercy. God, have mercy. Jesus, have mercy." I was his pastor and also a good friend.

I smiled when I heard him tell the story because I had forgotten that phone call. Then it all came back to me. My answer was off the top of my head, but in retrospect it was perfectly biblical. Many times in life the only thing we can do is to cry out, "God, have mercy. Lord, have mercy. Jesus, have mercy." When we pray "deliver us from the evil one," we are asking for God in his mercy to help us in our time of great need.

When we are tempted to sin, it is all too easy to respond by fighting our battles in the flesh. Sometimes we are easy prey for

Satan because we take him too lightly. And sometimes we give up too soon because we forget that Jesus himself is praying for us. The Victor is praying that his victory might eventually be ours. That ought to give us enormous comfort in the heat of the battle. The God who calls us will give us whatever we need whenever we need it. The Lord has not brought us this far to cause us to fail. Fear not, child of God. Even your darkest moments are part of God's plan for your life. Before the story is finally told, our prayers will be answered, and we will be delivered from the evil one once and for all. Until then, stand and fight. The Lord is on your side.

GOING DEEPER

1. "The battle is half-won if you want to avoid temptation enough to beg God to help you." Why is it important to pray before we are tempted? What happens to us spiritually when we neglect this step?

2. In what way does Satan serve God's purposes in the universe? What happens when we attribute either too much or too little power to Satan and the demons?

3. If Jesus knew all about Peter's denials in advance, why didn't he try to stop him? How did God use this humiliating experience to refine Peter spiritually?

4. Read Romans 8:34; Hebrews 7:25; 1 John 2:1–2. What do these verses teach about the present ministry of Christ on behalf of all Christians? What encouragement can we take from the intercession of Christ in heaven?

PRAYER

Almighty God,

Forgive us for fighting our battles in the flesh.

Forgive us for taking Satan so lightly as to think that we are an even match for him.

Teach us to trust in you completely, to believe that Jesus Christ has won the victory, and to move from victory unto victory.

Teach us to pray, "Lead us not into temptation," that we might eventually be delivered from the evil one.

Amen.

5. Consider the three reasons given in this chapter that God sometimes lets his children go over the cliff and hit the bottom hard. How have you experienced this in your own life? Where did you see the grace of God in the midst of it all?

6. Do you agree that God intends to forgive our future sins even though we haven't committed them yet? Is this biblical? Does this give us a "license to sin" because we know we'll be forgiven anyway? What's wrong with that line of thinking?

AN ACTION STEP

Your friend Charlie left the ministry because of an embarrassing moral failure that nearly destroyed his marriage. After two difficult years of restoration, he feels ashamed, unworthy, and useless to the Lord. He struggles mightily with anger and despair. Using Peter's story as a reference point, how would you counsel Charlie? What lessons does he still need to learn? What hope can you give him that the Lord still loves him and still has a "hope and a future" (Jer. 29:11) for him?

A TRUTH TO REMEMBER:
The God who forgives our past and our present intends to forgive our future as well.

"For yours is the kingdom
and the power and the glory forever. Amen."
MATTHEW 6:13

CHAPTER TEN

PRAYING FROM THE FOOTNOTES

Before we begin: Why does the Lord's Prayer end with these words? What does this teach us about God? About our own limitations? About our need to pray?

WE COME NOW TO THE FINAL phrase in the Lord's Prayer: "Yours is the kingdom and the power and the glory forever. Amen." Immediately we are faced with a problem. This benediction is not in the text of some modern translations of the Bible. And yet we all know that these words are part of the Lord's Prayer. We know it because when we sing the Lord's Prayer, these words are always included. What's going on here? If these words are part of the Lord's Prayer, why aren't they in the Bible? If these words aren't part of the Lord's Prayer, who made them part of the musical text?

To put it simply: What happened to this part of the Lord's Prayer? The answer is as simple as the question: Some people think Jesus never said these words. They believe the Lord's Prayer actually ends with the words, "But deliver us from the evil one." No benediction. No amen. Where, then, did this benediction come from? These same people suggest that the early church felt that the prayer ended abruptly, so they added these words later. But this is not a huge problem because these words actually are in your Bible.

If you use the King James Version, the New King James Version, or the Holman Christian Standard Bible, these words are in the text as part of Matthew 6:13. In some other translations these words are in the footnotes or in the margin of the text. Virtually every modern translation includes them in one of those two places. But all of this is confusing to the modern reader of the Bible. After all, if the experts can't agree among themselves, how are we to come to any safe and sure conclusion? Is this benediction original or not?

WEIGHING THE EVIDENCE

To ask that question is to enter the fascinating world of textual criticism. Textual criticism is the study of the various ancient manuscripts of the New Testament in order to determine which readings are original. Most people realize that since there were no printing presses in the days when the New Testament books were written, each copy had to be written by hand—on papyrus, parchment, or some other material. Inevitably, when copies are made by hand, mistakes will creep in. Then when copies of the copy are made, the mistake will be repeated, and other mistakes and omissions will occur.

The problem is complicated by the fact that literally thousands of copies of the New Testament were written over hundreds of years, in many different languages, in many different places. Some of the copies are ancient, while others were made as late as one thousand years after the time of Christ. Furthermore, we have the sermons and letters of the early church fathers which themselves quote Scripture, and those quotations can be compared with what the various manuscripts say. All in all, textual criticism is a complex field led by a few specialists who bury themselves in ancient manuscripts, poring over the evidence and making their conclusions. The rest of us read the books they write and then make our own conclusions.

The one thing we know for certain is that this benediction does not appear in Luke's version of the Lord's Prayer, but it is found in many manuscripts of Matthew's new version of the Lord's Prayer. How do we account for these two facts?

It seems likely that Jesus taught this prayer to his disciples on more than one occasion, and he did not use the same word-for-word form. Everyone agrees that Luke's version omits the benediction. This seems to me to be a key point. The benediction *may* be original in Matthew; it is definitely *not* found in Luke.

Incidentally, the fact that Jerome, and thus the Latin Vulgate, omits the benediction explains why Catholic Bibles omit the benediction (usually without even a footnote). It also explains why Catholics are sometimes surprised when they visit an evangelical church and discover that we have "added" something to the Lord's Prayer.

A POSSIBLE SOLUTION

Let me say frankly that I lean toward the view that Jesus originally spoke these words. We know that Jesus often repeated his teachings. We know that he was not bound by any need to repeat himself word for word. He may have added the benediction on some occasions, and on other occasions he may have omitted it. I think it is likely that Matthew's version including the benediction is correct, and Luke's version that omits it is also correct.

If some such reconstruction is not true, then it is hard to understand why the benediction was added to one version and not to the other. After all is said and done, no one can say with certainty that Jesus did or did not say these words. The matter is not totally closed either way. I think he said them at least once when he taught the Lord's Prayer. I also think he sometimes omitted these words. And I think the manuscript evidence reflects those two traditions.

I regard the benediction as the legitimate words of Jesus. Everyone agrees that the words are both true and biblical (King David used similar words in 1 Chronicles 29:11–13). They form a fitting end to the Lord's Prayer. In fact, it would be difficult to compose a more fitting conclusion.

Let us proceed then, assuming that these words may indeed be original and are at least true and biblical. If Jesus did say these words, what do they add to our understanding of the Lord's Prayer? I suggest that they teach us three important truths.

GOD—SOURCE OF ALL BLESSINGS

First, these words point us back to God as the source of all our blessings. There is a trinitarian emphasis in this closing benediction that reinforces both halves of the Lord's Prayer. Notice how perfectly the benediction brings the whole prayer together: We are to pray that God's name might be "hallowed" for "yours is the glory." Thus even our "daily bread" is made sacred when we eat it to God's glory. We are taught to pray, "Your kingdom come," and to say, "Yours is the kingdom." And it is by the grace of King Jesus that our sins are forgiven. We are taught to pray, "Your will be done" because "yours is the power," and it is by the power of the Spirit that we are rescued from Satan's control.

By arranging the prayer this way, Jesus is teaching us one of the fundamental truths of the Christian life: *All our blessings ultimately come from God.* No realm of life lies outside the realm of prayer because *everything* we receive comes as a gift from our loving Heavenly Father. Our prayers are not only to be addressed to God; they are also to be founded in God. We are to rest our hopes in him alone and not on our clever schemes and human designs. We like to think that God is lucky to have us on his side; the Lord's Prayer teaches us how lucky we are to be on his side. He could do just fine without us. We couldn't survive for a moment without his sustaining grace.

All that we are and all that we have comes from God. Everything is a gift. Nothing is earned; everything is given.

- Your life is a gift.
- Your health is a gift.
- Your career is a gift.
- Your intelligence is a gift.
- Your strength is a gift.
- Your personality is a gift.
- Your children are a gift.
- Your friendships are a gift.
- Your possessions are a gift.
- Your accomplishments are a gift.
- Your wealth is a gift.

You own nothing. *Everything you have is on loan from God.* He gives it to you for a little while and says, "Take care of it." We hold on tight because we think it all belongs to us. Sooner or later we'll understand that it doesn't belong to us, and it never did.

We are like little children holding so tightly to a few borrowed marbles. *We grip them in our palm because we're afraid of losing them.* But sooner or later God himself begins to pry the marbles out of our hand. One by one he pulls our fingers off the things we think are ours. We may fight back, but he is stronger, and he always wins. In the end he takes back that which belongs to him in the first place.

Life is the ultimate gift, but none of us lives forever. Rich man, poor man, beggar man, thief. Man, woman, boy, girl, white or black, young or old, unknown Christian or Roman Catholic cardinal—we all die sooner or later.

"IT DOESN'T GET ANY BETTER THAN THIS"

Several of my friends are about to make job changes and major career moves. In more than one case it means leaving this area for another part of the country; sometimes it means leaving a job with no certainty about a future paycheck. Since I've been in both situations myself, I know how unsettling it can be.

Many years ago my friend Jerry Hansen gave me a piece of advice for handling moments like this. The human tendency is to look at change as bad and to value stability above everything else. It's true that moving to Montana (or wherever) is going to mean an abrupt change in scenery, and it probably also means you're going to have to start at ground zero making new friends, finding a new church, and putting your children in a new school. That's not easy, and it won't happen overnight. It may take months or even a year or two before you truly feel settled and "at home" again.

When I was between jobs and more or less drifting along in thin air, Jerry took me out to eat one day and told me something like this: "Ray, you need to enjoy this part of your life. If you fight what God is doing, it will just take things longer to work out. But if you relax and let God lead you, eventually you'll look back and see God's hand every step of the way." Then he gave me the punch line: "Don't forget. It doesn't get any better than this." I still smile years later when I think of those words because he was absolutely right. How many hours (days? weeks? months?) do we waste fretting over our circumstances and dreaming of better days when all our problems will be behind us? In truth, those "better days" never really come—not perfectly, not in a fallen world where nothing works right all the time.

Is there a theological truth behind this? Absolutely. If God is God, then he is just as much the God of your cloudy days as he is the God of bright sunshine. While reading my personal journal this week, I happened across a quotation I recorded two years ago: "You can't push a river. You've got to let it flow." God's work in your life is like a river flowing steadily toward its appointed destination. Right now your "river" may seem to have taken a detour, and you may feel like trying to rush the current along. It can't be done. The river can't be rushed.

Are you worried about your future? Fear not. Don't rush the river. Enjoy these days as part of God's plan for your life. Go with the flow, and soon enough God will bring you into a safe harbor. Enjoy the blessings of today, and remember that everything good comes from God.

KEEP GOING

Second, these words teach us to keep on going in hard times. Just consider these three statements:

1. *God rules the governments of this world.* That's the approximate meaning of the phrase, "Yours is the kingdom." The kingdom belongs to God. He is the ruler over the affairs of men. Governments come and go, nations rise and fall, presidents and prime ministers rise to power and then suddenly disappear. Men plot to overthrow, and then suddenly they themselves are overthrown.

I recall the week in 1991 when Communism finally ended in Russia. On Monday morning we awoke to the news that Gorbachev had been overthrown. Then we saw pictures of Boris Yeltsin standing on the tanks, rallying the people. One of the cable news networks was there, broadcasting the news to the entire world. On Monday night word spread that the Communists were going to storm the Russian Federation building. On Tuesday the people defiantly declared they would never go back to Communism. Then on Wednesday the coup leaders had flown away from Moscow in utter desperation.

Wild celebrations. Hundreds of thousands of people dancing in the streets. The old Russian flag unfurled. Then the most impossible things happened. Hundreds of young Russians gathered in Dzerzhinsky Square directly outside the KGB headquarters, pulling down the huge statue of the evil Felix Dzerzhinsky. Just four months earlier I walked right past that statue in Moscow. If anyone had tried to pull it down then, they would have been shot. But in a matter of a few days, the Communist regime had come to a sudden end. Then Latvia and Estonia joined Lithuania in proclaiming their independence. Then Gorbachev returned. Then the world welcomed Yeltsin as a hero. And then the Communist Party was effectively outlawed.

The world turned upside down in less than a week.

As I thumbed through my copy of *The Great Thoughts* by George Seldes, I came upon these words of V. I. Lenin: "Religion is the opium of the people. Religion is a kind of spiritual vodka in which the slaves of capitalism drown their human shape and their claim for any decent life."[1]

For seventy years the Communists tried to a build a paradise on earth by following Lenin's words. They truly thought they could stamp out religion from Russian life. But today Communism is a dead corpse waiting to be buried in the graveyard of history. Meanwhile, the church of Jesus Christ is stronger than ever.

That's not all Lenin said. Listen to these brave words: "Give me four years to teach the children and the seed I have sown will never be uprooted."[2]

Eighty years have passed, and Lenin's face lies in the dust. Even the great city named for him has reverted to its historic name—St. Petersburg. Lenin's prophecy was a failure because his seed bore nothing but rotten fruit. And the crowning irony is this: Only among the older generation can you find anyone who still follows Lenin. The young people know they were lied to, but the church rolls on. The hammer and sickle has come down, but the church rolls on. They are tearing down the statues of Lenin, but the church rolls on. The Communists are out of a job, but the church rolls on. The mighty Soviet Union is no more, but the church rolls on—not just the church universal, but the church in Russia. That church—evangelical and Bible-believing, persecuted, hated, jailed, vilified, maligned, mocked, ridiculed—is rolling on today, stronger than ever. Tempered by years of suffering, purified through decades of tribulation, unified through persistent prayer, held together despite all that Lenin and Stalin and the rest could do. *That* church is rolling on. When you look at a map of the former U.S.S.R., remember the lesson: *God rules the governments of the world.* "Yours is the kingdom."

2. *God has the power to support his people.* That's the second part of this great benediction, "Yours is the power." Whatever his children need, the Heavenly Father can supply. Do they need wisdom? He *is* wisdom. Do they need strength to carry their burdens? He has an unlimited store. Do they need power? His are the hands that created the universe. Do they need mercy? His mercies are new every morning. Do they need material supply? He owns the cattle on a thousand hills.

The whole Bible is a testimony to this great truth. Where God guides, God supplies. He will never lead his children where he cannot meet their needs.

There is no power shortage with God. He has the power to support his people no matter how difficult their trials may be.

I've known Steve and Liz Massey for almost twenty years. Steve was an elder of the church I pastored in Texas, and Liz often sang solos during our worship services. Their children attended Awana with our children. We lost touch when we moved to Oak Park in 1989. About nine years ago Steve came through Chicago on business, and we ate supper together. I was surprised to learn that he had started writing poetry, and I recall that he sent me a poem about my youngest son and one of his friends. Then in 1996, we traveled through Dallas and saw Steve and Liz at a reunion of folks from our old church. That's when I learned that Liz had been having some serious health problems. A few months ago Steve wrote to say that Liz needed a kidney transplant and that their son Aaron was going to donate one of his kidneys to his mother.

After the operation Steve sent me a small book of poems he had written called *Plans for You.* At a low point he wrote a poem called "The Author of Miracles." It included these words:

"We need a miracle now
a band-aid or aspirin won't do
'cause we need a miracle now.

Not a walk on water
or mountain in the sea miracle
but a healing from you.

We've so little faith somehow
but since all power resides in you
that's where we'll rest now.

Lord, we've just found out
that we need a miracle now
so we send up our request
and rest in you now."

Evidently the miracle came in one form or another because the surgery was successful, even though Liz's body keeps trying to reject Aaron's kidney. The battle continues; the war is not over. In a recent note he commented that trials are difficult mostly because we don't know when (or if) they will end. Then he added this thought: "Liz and I are beginning to appreciate Job. He kept getting sicker and sicker, yet he refused to curse God and die. (I'm working on a spoof piece dedicated to our choir entitled, 'The More You Pray, the Sicker We Get.') Trials are not about time. They are not about double blessings you might get if you endure as Job did. (If Job had bugged out one day early, would he have received anything from God? How many Christians bug out of their college/business/marriage one day early?) Trials are about God. Illness happens because life happens. So you're having a bad year. So! Who's in charge?"

"Trials are about God." What a good thought that is. God is large and in charge. He sees what is hidden to us. We have chosen to believe even when we cannot see, and in that faith we find the strength to face each new day. When we pray, "Yours is the power," we affirm our confidence that God will give us whatever we need, in good times and in hard times, and that even in our trials God's strength is made perfect in our weakness.

3. *All that God does, he does for his glory.* "Yours is the glory." All that God does *for* us, all that God does *in* us, all that God does *through* us, all that God does *with* us, he does for his glory. And what is the glory of God? It is anything that enhances God's reputation in the world. This is a crucial principle to remember when we pray. It's the key to understanding why some prayers are answered in ways that greatly surprise us. *All his answers are for his glory. God never answers prayer in any way that does not ultimately bring glory to his name.*

Sometimes God's glory is enhanced through a miraculous answer to prayer. Other times God is glorified when his children endure suffering patiently. Sometimes God allows a teenager to drift away from him despite the prayers of that teenager's parents. Why? In part because God respects the freedom of the human will. He will not compel people to serve him. And in part because God will receive greater glory through the repeated prayers of the parents as they model consistent faith in the face of a great family difficulty. And finally, God may allow it so that when the teenager finally returns to them, they will glorify God for his discipline while he was in "a far country."

This principle applies to all the areas of life. Sometimes God is glorified through our prosperity and sometimes through our poverty. Sometimes his reputation is enhanced when we get the job for which we prayed, sometimes when we react in a godly manner even though we lose our job. In all things God is working to bring glory to himself through the lives of his obedient children.

He will do whatever is best for our ultimate spiritual good. And in the end we will discover that whatever was for our ultimate spiritual good also ultimately brought glory to his name.

There will be good times and bad times, miraculous deliverances and long seasons in the desert, happiness and sadness, popularity and misunderstanding. All the emotions and experiences of life are included in the things God uses to bring glory to his name. A friend E-mailed me with the news that his mother's cancer surgery had been successful. He ended his message with this statement: "God is God, good and great." As I pondered his words, I was struck at once by their simplicity and profundity. How much truth those six little words contain. They summarize an entire Christian worldview.

To say that God is God is simply to remind ourselves of the first rule of the spiritual life: He's God, and we're not. When I read my Bible, I seem to find it everywhere—popping up on every page and in every biblical story. Because God is God, he does whatever pleases him and works in every situation of life in ways I cannot see and would not understand if I could see. This is a humbling truth because it brings me to my knees and forces me to admit that he alone is running the universe, and I'm not running any part of it—not even the part I think I'm running.

To say that God is good means that his heart is inclined toward kindness. This gives me courage to pray for mercy in times of trouble. It also helps me to keep a positive perspective when life tumbles in around me. We often say that all things work together for good—and they do (Rom. 8:28)—but that's true only because God himself is good. He has promised to provide my every need, and because he is good, he will keep that promise. That means I can be content right now because I have everything I need at any given moment. If I truly needed anything else, God would give it to me.

To say that God is great means that he isn't limited by my circumstances but can work through them for my good and his glory. A sixty-nine-year-old woman I've never met wrote me from Florida. Through decades of suffering she never lost her faith—or her sense of humor. Here is how she put it: "If not for the grace of God, forget it. Miracles one after another. Awareness of Christ in my life. It blows my mind." What a wonderful testimony from one who has discovered God's greatness in the midst of her pain.

Let these six simple words lift your spirits: "God is God, good and great." God is God; be humbled. God is good; be encouraged. God is great; be thankful. When we pray, "Yours is the glory," we are declaring that Romans 8:28 is true. God is at work in all things for our good and his glory.

PRAISE GOD

Third, these words teach us to praise God always. When we pray, we are to begin by asking that God's name be hallowed, and we are to end by praising God for his sovereign rule over the affairs of men. Thus the prayer begins with God and ends with God. God is its subject and its object. He is the one to whom the prayer is addressed, and he is the source of every answer that flows to humankind.

Matthew Henry said, "Praise is the work and happiness of heaven, and all who go to heaven hereafter, must begin their heaven now." We are to praise God not because he needs it but because he deserves it and because we need to do it. Praise fits us to receive God's blessings now and to enter God's presence later. It is the highest work of mortal man, for it lifts man from the mundane and points him toward the sublime. Praise redirects our vision from the temporary to the eternal. Psalm 71:14 says, "I will praise you more and more." So let us, when we pray, remember this great lesson. Let us fill our prayers with praise to God. It is only right that we should do so, seeing that we are recipients of so many heavenly blessings.

Several years ago I was in Dallas for several days doing a series of radio interviews for a book I had written. I was doing a live television interview that was going smoothly until the host asked me a question that had nothing to do with my book. He leaned over to me and asked, "What's God been teaching you lately?" That's not an easy question under any circumstances, but it's doubly tough when the camera is staring in your face. I thought for a moment, then gave a simple reply: "I've been learning lately that I've still got a lot to learn about God." That may seem elementary, and in a sense it is, because no matter where you are in your spiritual life, you're still far from knowing God in all his fullness. Several times recently the thought has occurred to me that even though I've been a pastor for almost twenty-five years, there is still so much I don't know about God. At this point in my life, I'm more aware of what I don't know than what I do know.

"IS GOD GOOD?"

If I had to hazard a guess, I would say that my number one lesson in the past twelve months has been primarily about God's goodness. I don't think a day has gone by that the question, Is God good? has not been on my mind. In the churches of Nigeria, when the pastor cries out, "God is good," the congregation replies in unison, "All the time!" They repeat it over and over, each time proclaiming that "God is good . . . all the time."

Do we really believe it? As I write these words, there is news of the kidnapping of missionaries in the Philippines and a report about the startling spread of AIDS in Africa. In one country the rate of infection is an astonishing 36 percent. How do you explain the goodness of God to the families of those who are dying of this terrible disease? A woman I hardly know told me that after twenty-seven years of marriage her husband decided he didn't want to be married anymore. So they have separated, and now he says he never loved her in the first place. To make matters worse, he looked her in the face and said, "There is absolutely nothing at all I find attractive about you." Did I mention that he is a pastor?

When we hear about parents killing children and children killing parents, about high-level corruption and drive-by shootings, when families break up and children are abandoned, we want to cry out, "Where is God?" What does it mean to say, "God is good all the time" in those situations?

GOD OF THE GOOD TIMES

Some of us have constructed a God of the good times. When our prayers are answered and life is going our way, we say, "God is good." Does that mean when our prayers are unanswered and the cancer returns that God is no longer good? If your God is only good during the good times, then your God is not the God of the Bible.

A few years ago our oldest son and a few friends survived a terrible crash in our van that sent all of them to the hospital and nearly cost them their lives. During a Thanksgiving morning worship service, my wife stood and said something like this: "We are grateful that God spared our son and his friends. Many people have said, 'God was certainly good to you.' Ray and I believe that with all our hearts. But I want to say that even if our son and his friends had died, God would still have been good whether we understood it or not."

While I confess that I believe every word is true, I was unnerved when she said it. As I have pondered the matter since then, I have concluded that faith is not a feeling based on our circumstances. True biblical faith is conscious choice to believe that God is who he said he is and that he will do what he said he will do.

Sometimes you choose to believe because of what you see; often you believe in spite of what you can see. As I look to the world around me, many things remain mysterious and unanswerable. But if there is no God, and if he is not good, then nothing at all makes sense. I have chosen to believe because I must believe. I truly have no other choice. Along with millions of believers across the centuries, I have learned through my tears that my only confidence is in God and God alone.

The final two words of the Lord's Prayer say simply, "Forever. Amen." Don't go quickly past those two words. *Forever* tells us the *duration* of the benediction, and *Amen* teaches us the *certainty* of the benediction. Thus all the great themes of the prayer come together in one triumphant climax. Write these truths in your heart, for they are always true and will never change.

- We pray because we *know* these things are true. "Yours is . . . Yours is . . . Yours is . . ."
- We pray because we know these things are *always* true. "Forever."
- We pray because we know these things are always true, and we should *say so*. "Amen."

GOING DEEPER

1. Why is it important to remember that all our blessings come from God? What happens when we forget this vital spiritual truth?

PRAYER

Gracious Father,

When we are tempted to despair because of situations that seem out of control, help us to remember that "yours is the kingdom."

When we feel like giving up in the face of impossible difficulties, remind us that "yours is the power."

And when we become too impressed with ourselves, teach us again that "yours is the glory."

With the people of God across the ages, we affirm that these things are always true.

Amen.

2. "You can't push a river. You've got to let it flow." In what areas of your life are you trying to "push the river" instead of letting it flow?

3. "Trials are not about time. Trials are about God." How has God revealed himself to you through your difficulties and personal struggles?

4. "God is good . . . all the time." What evidence would you bring both for and against that statement? How does the cross of Christ demonstrate the goodness of God?

5. Psalm 100:4 exhorts us to come into God's presence with thanksgiving and praise. Take a moment to sing your favorite hymn or chorus as an offering of praise to the Lord.

6. As you look back over your study of the Lord's Prayer, what have you learned about God? Prayer? Yourself?

A TRUTH TO REMEMBER: ***When we pray, "Yours is the power," we affirm our confidence that God will give us whatever we need, in good times and in hard times and that even in our trials God's strength is made perfect in our weakness.***

AN ACTION STEP

Read Psalm 103 out loud. Take fifteen minutes to make a "Good News about God's Goodness" list. List the ways you have seen the goodness of God in the last twelve months. Post your list where you can see it every day. Use the list as a means of encouragement when you feel that God has forgotten you.

A FINAL WORD

THE LORD'S PRAYER REVISITED

WE COME NOW TO THE END OF OUR study of the Lord's Prayer. As I end this book, I go away with a profound appreciation for these words of Jesus. My own walk with God has greatly benefited by pondering the deeper meaning of the Lord's Prayer. As we wrap things up, let me repeat again that the Lord's Prayer answers the question, What does Christian prayer look like? Truly Christian prayer starts with God, moves to our human needs, and rises to God again. As we learn to pray the Lord's Prayer with understanding, we journey to the heart of our Heavenly Father. Jesus gave us this simple prayer so that starting from wherever we are on planet Earth, we can instantly travel to the throne room of the universe. There we come face to face with the one who loved us and gave his Son to redeem us. We call him Father, and he welcomes us as dearly loved sons and daughters.

Every word in this prayer is important. Nothing is added as filler. Nothing is unimportant. Every word adds to the meaning of the whole. It is truly the model prayer for the followers of Jesus.

The word *Our* reminds us that we do not pray alone but in fellowship with God's people scattered around the world.

We pray to our *Father* who loved us and gave his Son for our salvation.

We affirm that Our Father is *in heaven,* where he reigns supreme over the entire universe.

We ask that God's name be *hallowed* by the way we live so that others will look at us and give glory to our Father in heaven.

We are praying both for the king and the *kingdom to come,* and while we wait, we pray for courage to be "kingdom people" who reflect the values of the world to come.

We pray for *God's will to be done,* even if it means that our will is not done.

We acknowledge that God's will is not yet *done on earth as it in heaven,* but we do our part by sharing the gospel and showing forth the love of Christ to those we meet every day.

We pray for *our daily bread* because we depend completely on the Lord for what we need, and we share what we have with others because God has blessed us so richly.

We pray that *our debts might be forgiven* because we are sinners in thought, word, and deed.

We also *forgive our debtors,* knowing that we cannot have fellowship with the Father while we harbor bitterness in our hearts toward others.

We pray that God will *not lead us into temptation* because we realize our weakness, and we know that without God's help we will lose the battle every time.

We put on the armor of God by faith, asking God to *deliver us from the evil one.*

Because we believe that *yours is the kingdom,* we eagerly anticipate the day when the kingdoms of the earth will give way to the kingdom of the Lord Jesus Christ.

Because we believe that *yours is the power,* we do not give up in the face of difficult trials but instead live in faith that the Lord has a purpose and will give us whatever we need to face the challenges of each day.

Because we believe that *yours is the glory,* we have chosen to live for God instead of for the praise of men.

We confidently believe that these things are true *forever.*

Therefore, we say *Amen,* so be it, Lord.

LORD'S PRAYER PEOPLE

Now we are finished. Only one question remains: What difference will the Lord's Prayer make to you? Are you any different because you have read this book? Will it make any difference in the way you live? I wish someone would start a Lord's Prayer movement in the body of Christ. How much richer we would be if God's people would make this prayer central in their lives. How much stronger his church would be if all of us would pray this prayer every day. How much deeper our walk with God would be if we grasped what this prayer is saying to us. We would have more joy, more power, more strength, more wisdom, more of all the things we so desperately need.

Let me leave you with some specific suggestions. First, *pray the Lord's Prayer each day.* I don't mean simply to repeat it by memory, although that is certainly good. Pray it slowly, thoughtfully, pausing over each petition, pondering the words, rephrasing them until each petition becomes the desire of your heart.

Second, *try singing the Lord's Prayer.* You don't need to be a trained soloist, and you don't need an audience. You could sing the words while you walk or while you drive or while you ride an exercise bike. The music and the words together will tattoo this prayer on your soul.

Third, pray it with your children. Begin each day by praying the Lord's Prayer around the breakfast table. Let each child repeat a phrase until you have said the whole prayer. The brevity and cadence of the Lord's Prayer is so simple that young children can learn it even if they don't understand all the words. If your chil-

PRAYER

Lord Jesus,

We have your words before us.

How simple they are yet how profound.

It will take us a lifetime and more to comprehend them fully.

Thank you for making this prayer simple so that we could understand it.

Thank you for making this prayer profound so that we would never outgrow it.

May your words become our prayer so that your glory might become our goal.

Amen.

dren learn this prayer early on, they will not forget it when they are older.[1]

Fourth, *try praying this prayer for someone else.* The Lord's Prayer is a great guide to intercessory prayer. Begin by praying that God's name might be honored in that person's life, that they might submit their life to God's kingdom and God's will, and then go on from there. Every righteous thing that you could desire for any friend is contained somewhere in the Lord's Prayer.

Fifth, *teach it to someone else.* Use this book as a study guide. Read a chapter together and work through the questions. And don't forget to tackle the Action Step every week. While you're at it, go ahead and jot down notes, thoughts, observations, and questions in the margin of the book. I wrote this book to be used and not merely to take up space on a bookshelf. By teaching this prayer to someone else, you'll be helping at least two people—your friend and you. By the way, the Lord's Prayer would make an excellent study for a small group or a Sunday school class. It's also an excellent pattern for group prayer.

We'll know we've begun to learn what this prayer is all about when we become Lord's Prayer people. Those are the people who have taken this prayer off the pages of Holy Scripture and made it a part of their lives. They not only say this prayer but also believe it and live it and share it with others. God grant that we should all become Lord's Prayer people and so bring glory and honor to the one who taught us to pray in this way.

APPENDIX

SINGING THROUGH THE LORD'S PRAYER

LISTED BELOW ARE HYMNS, GOSPEL songs, and choruses that correspond to the various parts of the Lord's Prayer. I have found it helpful to sing my way through the Lord's Prayer using these songs to focus my thoughts. This list is meant to be suggestive, not comprehensive. As you use this guide, feel free to write down other hymns and choruses that help you draw near to the heart of God as you sing and pray your way through the Lord's Prayer.

OUR FATHER IN HEAVEN

All Creatures of Our God and King
Awesome God
Come, Thou Fount of Every Blessing
Crown Him King of Kings
Crown Him with Many Crowns
Father, I Adore You
He's Got the Whole World in His Hands

Hosanna
How Great Thou Art
I Love You, Lord
I Worship You, Almighty God
Now Thank We All Our God
O God, Our Help in Ages Past
Rejoice, Ye Pure in Heart
Worthy, You Are Worthy

YOUR NAME BE HONORED AS HOLY

Ancient of Days
Come, Thou Almighty King
El Shaddai
Glorify Your Name
Great Is the Lord
Holy Ground
Holy, Holy, Holy
Immortal, Invisible
Majesty, Worship His Majesty
No Other Name
O Lord, You're Beautiful
O Come, All Ye Faithful
O Worship the King
Salvation Belongs to Our God
Shout to the Lord

YOUR KINGDOM COME

All Hail King Jesus
All Hail the Power of Jesus' Name
Celebrate Jesus
Christ the Lord is Risen Today
Emmanuel
He Is Exalted
He Lives
His Name Is Wonderful
I Love Thy Kingdom, Lord
I Love to Tell the Story

Jesus Is Alive
Jesus Loves Me
Jesus Shall Reign
Joy to the World
Lord, I Lift Your Name on High
Seek Ye First
The King is Coming
Thou Art Worthy
We Will Glorify

YOUR WILL BE DONE

As the Deer
Have Thine Own Way
I Surrender All
I Will Never Be the Same Again
Give Me Jesus
Just As I am
Lord, I Want to be a Christian
Make Me a Blessing
Only Trust Him
Open Our Eyes, Lord
Open the Eyes of My Heart, Lord
Softly and Tenderly
Take My Life and Let It Be
Wherever He Leads, I'll Go
Give Us Today Our Daily Bread
Be Thou My Vision
Children of the Heavenly Father
Come, Ye Thankful People, Come
For the Beauty of the Earth
Give Thanks
God is Good All the Time
God Is So Good
Good to Me
He Is Able
God Will Make a Way
Guide Me, O Thou Great Jehovah

His Eye Is on the Sparrow
It Is No Secret
Let Us Break Bread Together
There Is None Like You
This Is the Day
'Tis So Sweet to Trust in Jesus
What a Friend We Have in Jesus

FORGIVE US OUR DEBTS

Amazing Grace
At Calvary
And Can It Be
Cleanse My Heart, O God
Jesus Paid It All
Just As I am
Nothing but the Blood
O Sacred Head, Now Wounded
Purify My Heart
Refiner's Fire
The Old Rugged Cross
There Is a Redeemer
We are One in the Bond of Love
Were You There?
When I Survey the Wondrous Cross
Worthy is the Lamb

DO NOT BRING US INTO TEMPTATION

Be Thou My Vision
Change My Heart, O God
Cry of My Heart
Great Is Thy Faithfulness
He Leadeth Me
How Firm a Foundation
It Is Well With My Soul
I Want to Be Where You Are
I Will Sing of the Mercies of the Lord
Like a River Glorious

Living for Jesus
Power of Your Love
Search Me, O God
Spirit of the Living God
Trust and Obey
Turn Your Eyes upon Jesus

DELIVER US FROM THE EVIL ONE

A Mighty Fortress is Our God
I Have Decided to Follow Jesus
I Will Call Upon the Lord
Lead On, O King Eternal
Only by Grace
Onward, Christian Soldiers
Precious Lord, Take My Hand
Stand Up, Stand Up for Jesus
This Is My Father's World
To God Be the Glory
Victory in Jesus
Where Cross the Crowded Ways of Life
Who Is on the Lord's Side?

YOURS IS THE KINGDOM . . . POWER . . . GLORY

Blessed Assurance
Blessed Be the Lord God Almighty
Christ, We Do All Adore Thee
Doxology
For All the Saints
Glory Be to the Father
He Has Made Me Glad
I Could Sing of Your Love Forever
I'll Fly Away
Let Everything That Hath Breath
Mine Eyes Have Seen the Glory
Nothing Is Impossible
Shine Jesus Shine
Soon and Very Soon
Standing on the Promises

The Church's One Foundation
This Little Light of Mine
The Lord Bless You and Keep You
We Bring the Sacrifice of Praise
You Are My All in All
Amen

ENDNOTES

CHAPTER 1

1. Helmut Thielicke, *Our Heavenly Father,* tr. John W. Doberstein (Grand Rapids: Baker Book House, 1974 reprint), 13–14.

2. Ibid., 14.

3. I am indebted to a tape by R. C. Sproul entitled "If God Is Sovereign, Why Pray?" for many of these insights.

4. I would add that it often seems the case that the more something matters to us, the longer we will have to wait for the answer to come. This is very often true when we pray for our loved ones to come to Christ.

CHAPTER 2

1. Sermon by Victor D. Pentz, "Tugging on God's Heart," 6 August 2000.

2. Philip Graham Ryken, *When You Pray* (Wheaton, Ill.: Crossway Books, 2000), 53.

3. Sermon by Charles Haddon Spurgeon, "The Fatherhood of God," 12 September 1858.

4. R. Kent Hughes, *Abba Father* (Westchester, Ill.: Crossway Books, 1986), 18.

5. Tom Wells, "God's Fatherhood and Prayer," *Reformation and Revival Journal,* 7, no. 2 (Spring 1998): 84.

CHAPTER 3

1. Sermon by John Piper, "Hallowed Be Thy Name," 4 November 1984. Emphasis in original.

2. William Barclay, *The Beatitudes and the Lord's Prayer for Everyman* (New York: Harper & Row, 1975), 188–89.

3. Thielicke, *Our Heavenly Father.*

CHAPTER 4

1. William Barclay, *The Beatitudes and the Lord's Prayer for Everyman,* 193.

2. The quotes are from Haddon Robinson, *Focal Point,* 7:1, January-March 1987.

3. S. D. Gordon, *Quiet Talks on Prayer* (Chicago: Fleming H. Revell Co., 1904), 46.

4. Michael Youssef, *The Prayer That God Answers* (Nashville: Thomas Nelson Publishers, 2000), 82.

5. These four prayer areas are taken from Larry Lea, *Could You Not Tarry One Hour?* (Altamonte Springs, Fla.: Creation House, 1987).

CHAPTER 5

1. Jim Bakker, *I Was Wrong* (Nashville: Thomas Nelson, 1997), 236.

2. Rita Bennett, *Inner Wholeness Through the Lord's Prayer* (Tarrytown, N.Y.: Chosen Books, 1991), 83–84.

3. The entire testimony may be found on the Association of Baptists for World Evangelism Web site: www.abwe.org.

4. Alden Thompson, "Thy Will Be Done," *Signs of the Times,* November 1988, 28.

CHAPTER 6

1. Martin Luther, *Small Catechism,* tr. Robert E. Smith, 1994.

2. William H. Willimon and Stanley Hauerwas, *Lord, Teach Us* (Nashville: Abingdon Press, 1996), 73, suggest that the Greek word translated "daily" means something like "sufficient" or "enough."

3. Sermon by Ray C. Stedman, "When Prayer Becomes Personal," 15 March 1964.

CHAPTER 7

1. C. S. Lewis, *Fern-Seed and Elephants,* Walter Hooper, ed. (Glasgow: Fontana/Collins, 1975), 39–40. Cited in Kent Hughes, *Abba Father* (Westchester, Ill.: Crossway Books, 1986), 79–80.

2. John R. Rice, *The King of the Jews* (Murfreesboro, Tenn.: Sword of the Lord Publishers, 1955), 107.

3. John F. Walvoord, *Thy Kingdom Come* (Chicago, Ill.: Moody Press, 1974), 53.

4. Max Lucado, *The Great House of God* (New York: Walker & Company, 1997), 135.

5. Kenneth Winston Caine and Brian Paul Kaufman, *Prayer, Faith and Healing* (Emmaus, Pa.: Rodale Press, 1999), 136.

6. John R. W. Stott, *Christian Counter-Culture* (Downers Grove, Ill.: InterVarsity Press, 1978), 149.

7. For an excellent discussion of the power of true repentance, see Oliver W. Price, *The Power of Praying Together* (Grand Rapids: Kregel Publications, 1999), 119–30.

CHAPTER 8

1. W. Phillip Keller, *A Layman Looks at the Lord's Prayer* (Chicago: Moody Press, 1976), 135.

2. William Barclay, *The Lord's Prayer* (Louisville, Ky.: Westminster John Knox Press, 1998), 98.

3. C. S. Lewis, *Mere Christianity* (Glasgow: Fontana/Collins, 1955), 122.

4. Ron Dunn, *Don't Just Stand There, Pray Something* (Nashville: Thomas Nelson Publishers, 1992), 46–47.

CHAPTER 10

1. George Seldes, *The Great Thoughts* (New York: Ballantine Books, 1985), 240.

2. Ibid., 241.

A FINAL WORD

1. Kenneth Winston Caine and Brian Paul Kaufman, *Prayer, Faith and Healing*, 137.

SPECIAL NOTE

If you would like to contact the author, you can reach him in the following ways:

By letter: Ray Pritchard
Calvary Memorial Church
931 Lake Street
Oak Park, IL 60301

By E-mail: PastorRay@calvarymemorial.com

Via the Internet: www.calvarymemorial.com